A FAITH
Worth Believing in the Last Days

A FAITH
WORTH BELIEVING IN THE LAST DAYS

David R. Dombrowski

Lighthouse Trails Publishing
Roseburg, Oregon

A Faith Worth Believing in the Last Days
© 2024 Lighthouse Trails Publishing
(see back of book for publisher contact information)

All rights reserved. No part of this book may be reproduced, stored in a retrieval system, or transmitted in any form by any means, whether electronic, mechanical, photocopying, recordings, or otherwise without prior written permission from the publisher. Excerpts and quotes may be used with proper citation without permission as the US Fair Use Act allows. Scripture quotations are taken from the *King James Version* unless otherwise indicated.

Cover and interior design by Lighthouse Trails Publishing. Cover photo "The Crew," 1902. "Small sailing boat in rough seas." Painting in the Aberdeen Maritime Museum, Aberdeen, Scotland. From "Modern Masterpieces of British Art" [The Amalgamated Press Ltd., London, c1930]; from alamy.com; used with permission.

ISBN: 978-1-942423-73-7

Note: Lighthouse Trails Publishing books are available at special quantity discounts. Contact information for publisher in back of book.

Printed in the United States of America

Contents

Part I: A Faith Worth Defending 11

1/ My Journey Out of Catholicism 13
A Good Catholic Boy 13
Salvation—Out of My Grasp 14
Drafted! 17
A Christian Community Throws a Curve Ball 20
A Dangerous Bridge 23

2/ Setting Aside the Power of the Gospel 25
The Uniqueness of Christianity 26
Didn't the Gospel Work? 27
There Is Power 30
Cling to the Gospel 32

3/ Sound the Trumpet in the Midst of Apostasy 35
Tares in the Church 36
The Fig Tree Ripens 38
Bridgers and Silencers 39
A Very Real Spiritual Battle 42

4/ The Peace of God Versus the P.E.A.C.E. of Man 45
A Utopian Kingdom on Earth? 46
Unheeded Warnings 48
A Peace Not of This World 50
Pursuing Peace But Not God 51

Part II: A Faith Worth Protecting 55

5/ Signs & Wonders! Five Things You Should Consider 57
I. Setting Things Up With Great Delusion 57
II. Are All Signs and Wonders From the Same Source? 59
III. Preparing the Way . . . But For "Who"? 61
IV. Signs and Wonders—and a True Minister of God 63
V. The Purpose of Signs and Wonders 63

6/ Drugs, Meditation, & "A Fully Developed Spirituality" 69
"The Foolishness of God" 70
A Fully Developed "Spirituality" 72
A Deadly Direction 77
Babylon 78
Sweeping the World 80
"The Regeneration of the Churches" 80
In His Will or Abandoning Truth? 82

7/ Calvinism, Catholicism, Or Blessed Assurance 85
The True Nature or a Distorted View of God 87
A Powerful Yet Dangerous System 87
Earthly Wisdom and Foolish Philosophy 89
The Calvinist "Gospel" 93
Calvin's God Too Small 95
The Foundation 96
Is There Assurance of Our Salvation? 98
The Spirit of Antichrist 99
Blessed Assurance 100

8/ A Potter Looks at Romans 9 105
A Refutation 107
Designed by the Potter 110
A Stumbling Block for the Calvinist 113

9/ Legalism or License Versus the Treasure of Living Water 117
The Law, a Way of Salvation? 120
Now, a License to Sin? 124
That Well of Living Water 124

Part III: A Faith Worth Believing 129

10/ Hard Lessons in Discernment 131
Lessons in Harsh Criticisms 132
The Chosen: An Unpleasant Task in Discernment 134
A Lesson in Finding the Truth 137
A Lesson in Knowing Who We Are and Who He Is 138

11/ A Master Carpenter Builds His Church 141
Looking for a Carpenter 141
Finding a Master Carpenter 142
The Carpenter Shows the Way 144
The Carpenter and the Church 146
The Carpenter and the Purifying of the Church 149
A Carpenter Who Prepares Us for the Future 150

12/ Preparing For Perilous Times and Finding God's Peace in the Midst of Them 155
When Judgment Comes 156
Being Prepared 158
In the Shadow of His Wings 161

13/ How Much Does the Gospel Weigh? 165
An Immeasurable Price 167
"Science Falsely So Called" 168

14/ Neglecting to Test the Spirits 171
A Creeping Effect 172
Testing the Spirits 175
"The Voice of Love"—Is There a Need to Test the Spirits? . 175
Sarah Young's "Jesus"—The Voice of God? 176
What Is the Test? 178
A Moment of Truth With a Moment of Terror 180
Living Inside a Bubble 183
The Cost 184
Now Is the Time 186

15/ Guard Your Heart With All Diligence 187
Guarding Our Hearts When Fear Rules 188
Guarding Our Hearts From Becoming Hard 189
Where Our Treasure Lies 191

Epilogue: Psalm 23—The Faithfulness of God 197

Endnotes 205

Index 211

To Deborah

Part 1

A Faith Worth Defending

Chapter 1

My Journey Out of Catholicism

Over the years, I have encountered many Christians who wonder, "What's wrong with being Catholic? After all, they believe in the Cross; they believe Jesus is the Son of God. It can't be all that bad." If you are a Christian who has wondered about these things, this special testimonial report is for you.

A Good Catholic Boy

I was born and raised as a Roman Catholic, so I am writing of things I know about and lived with for over thirty years. From my earliest childhood, I had a hunger and a thirst for God. I largely attribute this to my mother who instilled in me the love and reverence for God that she had. Born and raised in Poland, she grew up Catholic, but when she was about thirteen years old, while kneeling in a chapel alone, she invited Jesus Christ into her heart to be Lord of her life. Just prior to this, she had lost both of her parents to mushroom poisoning. Jesus filled a void in her life that carried her through many difficult years. Years later, she shared with me that this must have been her born-again experience, though in the Catholic Church she had not heard of such terminology; altar calls and making decisions to receive Christ were totally alien to her experience.

The fact is, there has never been a place in the Catholic Church for evangelistic crusades and personal decisions because every child raised Catholic is brought up with the belief that he is automatically "Christian" because he was baptized as an infant. In years past, many Anabaptists were burned at the stake because they recognized the fallacy and false assurance associated with infant baptism.

I guess I could accurately say that my mother had a personal relationship with the Lord, not because of Catholicism but in spite of it. As in her case, few Catholics even realize or understand what Catholicism really teaches and how the actual doctrines and teachings are polar opposites to biblical Christianity. Yes, the Catholic Church does teach morals, as do most religions, but when it comes to salvation, the actual teachings hinder and prevent the lost from finding The Way.

Salvation—Out of My Grasp

As a little boy, I had a very firm belief in God, and I knew that Jesus Christ is the Son of God who died on the Cross for my sins. I grew up as a religious boy, but my consciousness of sin and my sense of guilt never escaped me. As I grew to adolescence and then adulthood, the realization of my own sinfulness haunted me all the more. I can still remember one snowy night in winter in Portland, Oregon when I was nineteen; although it was nearly midnight, I decided to go for a walk. The moonlit snow enabled me to see my way clearly, and looking up at the stars that night somehow made me feel in touch with God. I still remember saying out loud to God at that moment, "God, I believe if I were to die tonight, I would go to Hell; and if that is going to change, you're going to have to do something." This was one of those rare moments where I was completely honest with God and addressed Him in a manner other than the rote, memorized prayer I was taught in the Catholic Church.

My Journey Out of Catholicism

If one thing can be said for Catholicism, it can help foster a sense of guilt in a practicing Catholic. My church life consisted of confessing my sins to a priest on a weekly basis, then receiving "absolution" only to come back the following week riddled with sin and guilt again. I think few Catholics and even fewer Protestants actually know or understand the Catholic way of "salvation," yet it is still printed in the Baltimore Catechism that we are saved by our participation in the sacraments. Central to Catholicism, in fact its very focal point, is the sacrament of the Eucharist where it is believed that bread and wine are literally transformed into the body and blood of Jesus. The implications of this belief, although unbiblical, may seem innocent enough until one realizes that this practice is without question the very heart and core of the Catholic "gospel." In other words, your participation of this sacrament is what saves you. The point is that your salvation depends on something you do. It gives you a temporary and false sense of assurance until you sin again. In fact, according to Catholic teaching, one can never be assured of one's own salvation. To have such assurance is to be guilty of the sin of pride. And looking back on it now, such a conclusion makes perfect sense because if our salvation were based on our performance (i.e., participation in the sacraments), we would have something to boast about. So logically from that point of view, if we don't acknowledge or recognize our salvation, at least in theory we can be humble about it. But Paul saw the error in all this fallacious thinking when he penned the words:

> I said out loud to God at that moment, "God, I believe if I were to die tonight, I would go to Hell.

> For by grace are ye saved through faith; and that not of yourselves: it is the gift of God: Not of works, lest any man should boast. (Ephesians 2:8-9)

For the Catholic, the concept of salvation by grace through faith alone is nearly impossible to receive because rooted in the heart of man (and virtually all religions) is the idea that we must earn our way to Heaven. Now that Catholics are beginning to read their Bibles, they will sometimes quote other Bible passages, especially from James, to prove that we are, after all, still saved by works. Little do they realize that James was trying to explain what biblical faith really is. It is not an intellectual ascent but a full trust and commitment to our Savior that expresses itself in the way we live. If James were trying to say that our good works justify us, he would not have used the story of Abraham, Isaac, and the altar to make his point. Surely, Abraham was a man of unusual faith, but he did not pretend that he could find salvation through his own goodness, nor was his attempt to sacrifice Isaac on the altar an expression of goodness but rather of his faith in God alone.

> **Growing up as a Catholic, I had virtually no knowledge of the Scriptures because we were never encouraged to read the Bible.**

In my case, growing up as a Catholic, I had virtually no knowledge of the Scriptures because we were never encouraged to read the Bible on our own lest we should come up with our own interpretations. And here is the crux of the matter: Christians often make the mistake of thinking that because Catholics believe in Jesus and the Cross, everything is OK But the reality is that as a Catholic, I knew that Jesus had atoned for my sins on the Cross but that redemption was not freely available to me. In some way, I had to earn my right to the Cross. This belief of mine was rooted to the very core of my being from participating in thousands of Masses where Jesus is re-crucified for my sins again and again. This deep heart-felt belief of mine that fostered my ongoing guilt was unfortunately not misconstrued but one hundred percent Catholic and totally in line with Catholic teaching. Salvation was, therefore, something attainable but always uncertain and out of reach. It is no wonder that the highly acclaimed Mother Teresa of Calcutta, who spent her life ministering sacrificially to the poor and sick in India, spent her final hours in serious doubts of her own salvation.

> And every priest standeth daily ministering and offering oftentimes the same sacrifices, which can never take away sins: But this man, after he had offered one sacrifice for sins forever, sat down on the right hand of God . . . For by one offering he hath perfected for ever them that are sanctified. (Hebrews 10:11,12,14)

Drafted!

I was now twenty years old and had completed my second year of college. I had feared the Vietnam draft because I heard they were now drafting college students into the military, but now that I was twenty, I felt secure that I need not fear the lottery any longer. But then, I received my draft notice in the summer of '72. I saw this as God's judgment on me, but little did I know at the time that God was answering what I had said to Him on that starry night a few months earlier.

My time in the Army brought a drastic change to my life. It was the first time I was away from home. It also was my first experience in getting to know other people on a deeper level as I lived and worked with them. For the first time in my life, I met Christians who shared with me the Gospel. One of them even gave me a New Testament, which I did read as I had made the decision that I would use my time in the military to seek for and hopefully find God.

In contrast, having been sent to Germany, I witnessed the selfish and destructive lifestyle of most of the soldiers. In my unit, the majority of them got high on drugs at every opportunity. And drunkenness and prostitution were widespread too. But I was known as the straight guy. In fact, I was so disgusted by what I saw happening around me that I determined not to have one taste of alcohol while I was there. Some of the soldiers mocked me, though I tried to be amiable and live at peace with them. I still remember one soldier blowing marijuana smoke in my face because I would not get high with them.

But all the while, I knew that my heart was unclean, and I saw in these soldiers a reflection of the dirt in my own life and knew I was headed toward moral destruction. This made me all the more anxious to find the victory and peace I was witnessing in the lives of the Christians. It was at this very low point of my life that I realized again, like on that night beneath the stars, that without God's intervention, my life would go to ruins. Up until now, I thought I had the power to change myself, but I now realized I was continuing on a spiritual decline. I picked up a Gospel tract that one of my sergeants had given me and found that salvation is within easy reach of anyone who will acknowledge his own sinfulness and inability to save himself. The hard part was getting to the place of recognizing my need of a Savior. And the Catholic gospel of justification by grace through works had hindered me from finding Christ for years.

I should caution you that if you were to approach the average practicing Catholic with this chapter, they would either tell you that I was mistaught Catholic doctrine as a youth or things have changed since Vatican II. However, the truth is literally staring us in the face when we realize that the Catholic priest performs an unbiblical ritual in the Eucharist, and Catholic doctrine still says that our participation in this is what saves us. In fact, if you were to take the Eucharist out of the Catholic Mass, you would no longer have the Mass. And if you took the Mass out of Catholicism, you would no longer have the Catholic Church, and no priest can deny this.

My Journey Out of Catholicism

Some may say, well, perhaps the Catholic Church is right about the doctrine of Transubstantiation. Maybe the communion wafer and the wine literally do become the body and blood of Jesus—under false appearances of course. But if this were true, then Jesus would necessarily have been lying to his disciples when He told them He had been using a figure of speech; rather than using the earthly term "flesh" in the literal sense, He used the term to express spiritual truth.

> It is the spirit that quickeneth; *the flesh profiteth nothing*: the words that I speak unto you, they are spirit, and they are life. (John 6:63; emphasis added)

But let's just suppose for a moment that Jesus had answered his disciples in another way when they began to murmur, "this is a hard saying; who can hear it?" Then suppose Jesus answered their confusion by saying, "Oh yes, I really meant it literally. Eating my flesh is profitable and will give you spiritual life." Given this scenario, would the Catholic Church be right in the celebration of the Mass, where Christ is re-crucified daily on an altar? The answer is *no* because we would still be speaking of another gospel than the one each of the apostles preached. And this is the one key point I want to get across in this chapter: Our justification is by grace through faith alone, not by our participation in a ritual. Being born of the Spirit is what gives us life—eternal life. By the way, Nicodemus was also troubled when Jesus said to him, "Ye must be born again" (John 3:7). He could not understand how anyone could come out of his mother's womb twice. Jesus was always speaking of spiritual things, using earthly terms and parables to express His meaning, but man, being carnal, always misunderstood His meaning, and so it is today.

My time in the service ended shortly after I read that tract and received the Lord in full trust to be my Savior. In fact, I found the Lord about two months before I left the service. God had wrought a miracle in my life in just two years, and I came out of the Army a new man—thanks to God, of course. God also opened my understanding of the Scriptures, but I did not know where to find fellowship. Then, I found out about Catholic charismatic meetings in my area. It seems that a goodly number of Catholics had found the Lord at the tail end of the Jesus movement, and these meetings provided a place for fellowship. I still remember a discussion we had as to whether or not we should leave the Catholic Church. The consensus was that we should stay so as to be a light to those who are still lost. For this reason, I remained in the Catholic Church for a number of years. Finally, as my life was more and more transformed by the Word of God, I realized that staying was not accomplishing my hope of being a light to Catholics, and the best witness I could provide was to leave. While I do not judge those who stayed for the benefit of the lost, I want to point out a serious fallacy in this thinking because the Catholic Church is non-reformable. As I alluded to before, the sacrament of the Eucharist is another gospel, but to do away with it would be to do away with the whole structure of the Mass, and the Catholic Church would then cease to exist. I feel very sorry for those believing Catholics who decided to stay; it must be very difficult for them and awkward for them not to feel like hypocrites.

A Christian Community Throws a Curve Ball

At the tail end of my stay in the Catholic Church, I joined an evangelical Christian community. From the day I found the Lord, I was always intrigued by Acts chapter 4, where the first Christians "were of one heart and of one soul: neither said any of them that ought of the things which he possessed was his own; but they had all things common" (Acts 4:32). The whole idea of community seemed like a piece of heaven on earth. I joined the community with the determination to make it work, even if the task was difficult. And difficult it turned out to be. Oddly, when I became a Christian, I was soon identified by other believers as having a gift of discernment, but now in this community it seemed that the opposite became the rule for the day: if something bothered me, the leaders said it was because I was fighting against God.

My Journey Out of Catholicism

I remember testing out this attitude one day when our community took a few days vacation trip. Somehow, our vehicles got separated, and sitting across from the driver, I said in jest, "I think maybe we should turn left." His immediate reply was, "Okay then, I'm going to turn right." Although done in humor, this incident was a true reflection of the attitude the members of the community had toward me.

Then, the day came when some of the leaders announced that they were considering becoming Catholic—this was a decision they were making not just for themselves but for all of us. When I joined the community, it was non-denominational though its roots were in a Baptist church. It had begun as a recovery ministry for young people who had forsaken drugs and alcohol or just needed a place to live. The fact that these leaders were now entertaining thoughts about Catholicism came as a great disturbance to me, but not as a total surprise. I had witnessed over the years how some of the members seemed somewhat intrigued with the Catholic Church and with Catholic mystics like Henri Nouwen and Thomas Merton. I remember one Christmas Eve when three of the women decided they were going to attend midnight Mass. I overheard them the next day talking about how enjoyable an experience it had been.

The meeting where the leaders announced their move toward Catholicism was anything but enjoyable for me. It was like watching a mutiny in one of those old pirate movies but without the violence. The senior elder of the community strongly opposed our becoming Catholic by saying it did not represent who we were. But there were too many others who had already decided they wanted to move in this direction. The senior elder was immediately removed from the community as a "discipline," but as time proved itself, he never came back. The community very quickly spiraled into the web of Catholicism.

> The community very quickly spiraled into the web of Catholicism.

I remember the night a Catholic priest was invited to speak to the community about Catholicism. This priest was recognized as a leader in the renewal movement of the Pacific Northwest. On that night, he proclaimed a great number of things. Here are some of the key points he shared with us:

- What is Ecumenism? The Protestants do not know what ecumenism actually means to the Catholic Church. They think it means that the Protestants and Catholics can have fellowship together as co-equals. What it actually means is that the Protestants will eventually be reabsorbed into the Catholic Church.
- Protestant pastors have no power when they do a communion service. They only go through the motions, but nothing really happens. Only the Catholic priest has the power and authority to perform a communion service.
- Protestants are the lost brethren because they have rebelled against (forsaken) the one true church.
- A good Muslim, a good Hindu, and a good Buddhist are saved. They have more hope of getting into heaven than the Protestants.
- The Protestants have a false notion of evangelism. As I have just told you, people of other religions are already saved. But the Protestants need to return to the Catholic Church.

Hearing these things that night helped me realize that the Catholic Church, as an institution, is much worse than I had allowed myself to believe. Although hearing these things was not actually new to me, it did surprise me that a leader in a renewal movement, where Catholics and Protestants mingled together, had such a low regard for the Protestants and a whole different agenda.

Perhaps what was even more surprising was that these sincere Christians, whom I had loved, lived with, and worked with side by side for over six years did not challenge this priest with his heretical beliefs that night.

The community was moving full steam ahead toward becoming Catholic, but there were some practical issues that had to be dealt with. For example, the leaders of the community had made a covenant to stay together for life, but the senior elder was no longer with them. They brought this problem to this Catholic priest who had a ready answer. He told them that he had the God-given power to dissolve the covenant. He explained that becoming Catholic superseded anything else. Then there was the matter of what to do with me. They thought if they sent me to talk to this priest one-on-one, he could persuade me to return to the "mother church." But when it became apparent that I was not turning back, I was told that I must leave.

Other things happened in that community. Things got really hot at times; there were fights between members. Eventually two marriages broke up where in both cases, the husband left the community, but the wife and children stayed behind to become Catholic. One of these husbands later confessed to me that when I myself was removed from the community, he thought God was removing me because I was not a part of God's special remnant. But after *he* was kicked out, he realized that what was once a loving Christian community had become a cult.

Not long after I was removed, the community became fully Catholic. They remain so today.

A Dangerous Bridge

As I am writing these things, I am amazed to think how quickly the years have gone by. These events that seem like yesterday began over thirty-five years ago. And through all these years, while I felt my story needed to be shared, I have not wanted to publicly disgrace the members of the community who had been seduced into false teachings; hence, I have kept the community and its members nameless. But there is a reason I have felt compelled to share it. When the community was deciding to become Catholic, they were very excited because they felt that they were pioneers in going back to the mother church. They felt confident that many others would eventually follow their example. Today, I see that this is beginning to happen in large numbers. The community shared with some of their friends that they had grown spiritually as far as the Protestant church could take them, and if they were going to grow anymore, they would have to become Catholic. It is the same thing that is happening today. Many Protestant leaders are now standing up and proclaiming that we need to glean from the teachings and practices of the Catholic church. Particularly appealing to them is contemplative prayer or mysticism and the spiritual disciplines. There is no doubt in my mind that contemplative spirituality is a bridge, bringing Protestants "back" to the Catholic church. The emerging church movement is equally a bridge toward Catholicism, and the Purpose Driven movement has had a role in this as well.

Chapter 2

Setting Aside the Power of the Gospel for a Powerless Substitute

If I were to say to you that much of the church today has set aside the power of God, would you be shocked? After all, we live in a time where having the power of God in your life is a major theme preached from pulpits across the country. And book after book, sold in massive quantities, pour off the presses promising a special connection or intimacy with God that will revolutionize your life and make it more dynamic. Yet, I believe I can prove that in fact, the power of God is being laid aside, and I will tell you how.

Back in the late 1990s, our family was visiting various churches in search of a new home church, and we noticed how many pastors would begin their messages with a Scripture but then launch into a lengthy talk that can best be described as a teaching based on behavioral psychology. For many sitting in the pews, this type of message had much appeal as the seeker-friendly movement was really taking off, and teachings about building relationships seemed more paramount than building a relationship with God based on the Word of God. At any rate, the preaching of the Gospel seemed to be held in second place, thereby creating a condition in the church where conviction of sin and the preaching of the Cross waned, while teachings appealing to the masses became more palatable and popular. Increasingly, it became a capital sin to offend your audience in a seeker-friendly church, and seeing as the preaching of the Cross is an offense to those who are perishing, the Gospel was seldom heard in these churches that were increasing in numbers—of which many were still unsaved. A case in point that illustrates this is a couple who attended Saddleback Church for years, but the wife was troubled by the fact that her husband did not know the Lord during that entire time. Then they started attending a church that preached the Gospel on a regular basis, and the husband got saved in the first two weeks. Yet Saddleback and the Purpose Driven movement have grown exponentially over the years. Ironically, for that couple, hearing the Gospel for two weeks, beyond saving the soul of that husband, did more to enhance their marriage relationship than hearing a social gospel for years. Suffice it to say, there is an unusual power to transform lives for the better when the Cross is preached and the doctrines of repentance, justification by grace through faith, and being born and renewed of the Holy Spirit are expounded upon. But, then again, the preaching of the Cross is offensive to those who are perishing.

> Hearing the Gospel for two weeks ... did more to enhance their marriage relationship than hearing a social gospel for years.

The Uniqueness of Christianity

Let us pause for a moment and think about what makes Christianity uniquely different from the world's religions. Christianity teaches that man is sinful and God is holy; consequently, man is unable to save himself. Heaping up good deeds does not atone for the fact that man's sin has separated him from God.

Setting Aside the Power of the Gospel

Then Jesus came as a sin offering to atone for sin, thereby eliminating our separation from God. As we receive Him by faith as our Savior, our sins are forgiven and the Holy Spirit indwells and transforms us where we can rightfully say we have been born again. Jesus then is Lord over our lives as we continue to trust and yield our lives to Him (we will say more about that later). But the religions of the world all teach the opposite—that man is basically good and has the power within himself to live a life pleasing to God, and thereby through his good works is able to save his own soul. Unfortunately, when the preaching of the Gospel was set aside in favor of a more seeker-friendly social gospel, it seems that the armor of the church was also laid down, and much of the false teaching of the world's religions crept in.

Whatever happened to the Christian church? Those of us who are old enough to remember can recall the unrest of the 1960s including the Vietnam War and the Hippie movement. It was an era of a lot of experimentation not only with drugs but with eastern religions and varied lifestyles. Then came the Jesus Movement where many lives were transformed under the preaching of the Gospel. Many people forsook their old lives and habits. All over the land, the phrase "praise the Lord" could be heard, and Bible prophecy was so popular back then as countless numbers were considering that we could be in the last days. Yet, over time, the joy and excitement of that new era waned, and I have not heard an explanation why. Most likely, the answer does not lie in any one thing, but one thing in particular happened, and that again is the laying aside of the Gospel.

Didn't the Gospel Work?

Initially, multitudes of believers, in the exhilaration of the times, had a sense that their needs and expectations would be met by the Lord. But then stories of woe began to emerge at the tail end of the Jesus Movement. Many who had come to the Lord began to return to their old ways and habits. Some went back to drugs, others to deviant lifestyles. Still others, who thought they would find sure victory in the Lord, found they lacked the power within to overcome their life-controlling and destructive habits. Also, stories would arise . . . like the one where a trusted Sunday-school teacher had been molesting kids; and those bound by pornography never forsook it, or they returned to it.

Now the question is, if all of these negative things were happening or beginning to happen again, who or what was to blame? It seemed that multitudes had given the Gospel a good shot, but for many it was not working.

Let me tell you, there is a great undoing effect to those who try to live as Christians but find they are living in defeat. Then, too, hearing story after story of Christians, many of whom you may have known personally, falling to a defeated lifestyle is also most disconcerting. In either case, the conclusion for many must have been that the Gospel was not working—that it was powerless to transform lives. Hence, the preaching of the Cross has been stilled.

It has been estimated that at least fifty percent of American pastors view pornography (largely on the Internet) on a regular basis. These estimates may in fact be quite conservative when we consider how many are probably too ashamed or afraid to admit their addiction. Pastors with life-controlling habits such as this are also often faced with a dilemma of who to look up to for help as they are supposedly at the top rung of the ladder and expected to live flawless lives.

Then, when they go to preach on Sunday morning on the power of the Cross, they find that they cannot because they know their lives are marred by defeat. Likewise, the wives of these pastors go through an incredible hell as they feel both challenged and insulted by something that has now robbed them of their husbands' affection and devotion. One thing I might say in passing is that years ago I heard there was an agenda among the Communist party to destroy our nation, not by warfare, but from within by corrupting our morals largely through pornography. Now if the Communist party has not attempted this, then Satan certainly has, knowing that the husband is a key figure and a prime target in destroying the family unit.

What we find then is that the Gospel, both for pastors and their congregations, seemingly is not working. The natural recourse for this would be to blame God, but rather than do this, other avenues of finding victory in God are being explored. The fact of the matter is that once the Gospel has been determined to be powerless, there is a scrambling for answers and new teachings. Hence, with this in mind, one can see why such a flood of new teachings has cropped up today—whether it be practicing eastern mysticism via contemplative prayer, the re-emergence of the spiritual disciplines of the Desert Fathers, or the varied teachings of the emerging church.

Brian McLaren, in his endorsement on the back cover of Alan Jones' book, *Reimagining Christianity*, has this to say:

> It used to be that Christian institutions and systems of dogma sustained the spiritual life of Christians. Increasingly, spirituality itself is what sustains everything else. Alan Jones is a pioneer in reimagining a Christian faith that emerges from authentic spirituality.

These are the words of an emerging leader pointing to the work of another emerging leader and, in a nutshell, telling us that the power of the Gospel is dead, and we need to explore other options. And the options most commonly turned to are New Age and eastern meditative practices. What you get from these teachings is that in the core of every human being is a "divine center" (i.e., God himself), and if you tap into that through meditation, you will find your own divinity and have limitless power. Sadly, what Brian McLaren has to say in the above quote has become the running orders of many Christians who have forsaken dogma (doctrine) for experience. Rather than seeking sound teaching, they seek an experience or "anointing" that works for them and empowers their lives. But, all the while, as they are engaging in experience-based "Christianity," they are becoming further removed from the truth of Scripture.

There Is Power

The Bible affirms there is power for the believer. David sang these words after being delivered from the hand of Saul:

> God is my strength and power: and he maketh my way perfect. (2 Samuel 22:33)

In Psalm 62, David sings:

> God hath spoken once; twice have I heard this; that power belongeth unto God. (Psalm 62:11)

Then in Psalm 68, David says:

> O God, thou art terrible out of thy holy places: the God of Israel is he that giveth strength and power unto his people. (Psalm 68:35)

Without question, Scripture declares overcoming power to God's people; but then why are God's people lacking it and looking for it now?

We don't need to search very far for the answer to that question, for the answer can be found in the words of Paul:

> For I am not ashamed of the gospel of Christ: for it is the power of God unto salvation to every one that believeth; to the Jew first, and also to the Greek. (Romans 1:16)

Then in his Gospel, John says:

Setting Aside the Power of the Gospel

> But as many as received him, to them gave he power to become the sons of God, even to them that believe on his name. (John 1:12)

From both of these Scriptures, it is clear that God gives power to the believer for holy living—but that power is found in the Gospel to those who believe it.

Apparently, what has happened in the church is that there has been so much failure that believers have reckoned the Gospel to be powerless and have looked essentially to "other gods" for help.

Jeremiah speaks of our day when he says:

> **God has declared that His overcoming power is to be found in the Gospel.**

> But this thing commanded I them, saying, Obey my voice, and I will be your God, and ye shall be my people: and walk ye in all the ways that I have commanded you, that it may be well unto you. But they hearkened not, nor inclined their ear, but walked in the counsels and in the imagination of their evil heart, and went backward, and not forward. (Jeremiah 7:23–24)

Regardless of what our natural instincts may tell us, God has declared that His overcoming power is to be found in the Gospel. Yes, a struggle may ensue for a period of time, but that is all the more reason to hold fast to the Gospel because only in it can true and lasting victory be found.

In Romans chapters 7 and 8, Paul describes the inner turmoil that may ensue in a person's life as he struggles with sin. Theologians speculate if Paul was speaking of his own struggles, and if so, before or after his conversion. I believe that Paul was writing of both our struggles and his own struggles both before and after conversion. And the lesson learned is that once we become believers, we cannot go back to trying to live in victory in the flesh; just as it did not work before conversion, it will not work now. This is what is happening in the church today, and it will fail because victory can only be found in the power of the Gospel. We can never live an overcoming life in the flesh (i.e., our own strength). Our power and might is found in the Lord, and that is why Paul directs us in Romans to live in the Spirit:

> For if ye live after the flesh, ye shall die: but if ye through the Spirit do mortify the deeds of the body, ye shall live. (Romans 8:13)

And this is all a part of the Gospel message because when we receive Christ at conversion by trusting in His atoning work as a free gift, God imparts His Holy Spirit to us (Romans 8:9), and we are born again or "born of the Spirit" (John 3:6). The life of the Christian means death to self (the flesh) but also new life in the Spirit that enables us to bear the fruit of the Spirit. Have you ever wondered how you can bear the fruit of the Spirit if your life is not empowered and directed by the Spirit? Each day we need to allow Jesus to be Lord over our lives—and that means that just as we trusted Jesus to save us on the day we came to Him, we need to trust Him to guide our steps as we commit our way to Him. In other words, just as we trusted Christ to save us on the day we received Him, we need to continue to trust Christ to complete His work in us. Remember that we were purchased by God through the death of His Son, so our lives are no longer our own, but we belong to Him.

Cling to the Gospel

If you are a Christian and your life is full of struggle, do not forsake the Gospel, but cling to it more fully knowing that you are not strong, but God is strong. Whether it be facing temptation or being chased by life's circumstances (as David was chased by Saul), our power and victory is found in the Lord only and not in ourselves. Do

Setting Aside the Power of the Gospel

not ask the Lord to help you live the Christian life, but allow Him to live the Christian life in and through you. Eastern mysticism and the New Age teach that in the center of our being we will find God (and become God-like or Christ-like); Christianity teaches that in the center of our being we find a heart that is utterly wicked and deceitful. Have no dealings with the old nature, but be renewed in the Holy Spirit. Remember that God promised to make a new covenant with us, not written on stone tablets but engraved on our minds and hearts (Hebrews 8:10). This New Covenant has the power to transform the human heart. Before Jesus went to the Cross, He spoke of this when He said, "this is my blood of the new testament, which is shed for many for the remission of sins" (Matthew 26:28). Simply put, Jesus was leaving a testament or will that would take effect after His death—with His own blood serving as the stamp or seal validating that will. It is interesting to note that if you take your Strong's Concordance and look up the Greek word for "covenant" (like the one used in Hebrews 8:10 above) and compare it with the Greek word for "testament" (like the one just used by Jesus), it is exactly the same Greek word. Jesus' death on the Cross was not only that perfect sacrifice for sin, but it also sealed the covenant prophesied in Jeremiah 31 and repeated in Hebrews 8:10 that God would write His laws on our minds and hearts. This is the marvelous transformation that so many people are looking for but think the Gospel is too weak to provide; yet it is the only sure and true way to holy living. The Gospel is that new covenant, and it is available to us when we acknowledge that apart from Him we can do nothing. Jesus said:

> I am the vine, ye are the branches: He that abideth in me, and I in him, the same bringeth forth much fruit: for without me ye can do nothing. (John 15:5)

So, if we abide in the Vine (Jesus) we will be victorious in our quest to live the Christian life. Have nothing to do with substitutes to the Gospel message. God saves and transforms people His way and not our way. Any other way is futility and idolatry.

We are living in a time of mass deception and delusion. If you were to fall off a cliff and only had a rope to hold you, would you not hold onto that rope more tightly? That is what we must do with the Gospel. Jesus' death on the Cross purchased our salvation; we have also been bought by His blood, sealed in a new covenant, and His indwelling presence empowers us to live the Christian life. There is no other power to save!

> For the preaching of the cross is to them that perish foolishness; but unto us which are saved it is the power of God. (1 Corinthians 1:18)

> For the kingdom of God is not in word, but in power. (1 Corinthians 4:20)

> Now also when I am old and greyheaded, O God, forsake me not; until I have shewed thy strength unto this generation, and thy power to everyone that is to come. (Psalm 71:18)

Chapter 3

Sound the Trumpet in the Midst of Apostasy— The Enemy Is in the Camp

Over the past years, we have watched with a mixture of surprise and sadness how an apostate church has materialized before our eyes. It all began for us here at Lighthouse Trails when we met Ray Yungen in 2000.[1] Though we were not publishers back then, he shared with us his manuscript for *A Time of Departing*, which spoke of a coming apostasy in the form of mystical practices and "spiritual disciplines." Stirred by the content of that book, we agreed to help him find a publisher. But, at the time, we never imagined how relevant and prophetic that book would be nor how quickly this apostasy would flourish in the mainstream churches. Today, it is even difficult to find a church that has not been compromised or in some way influenced by this contemplative spirituality (usually through Spiritual Formation programs). Now e-mails, phone calls, and letters pour into our office telling how readers who either just discovered us or were at one time skeptical of our warnings are now shocked to see that these things have entered their churches.

Tares in the Church

How did this happen, and how did it happen so quickly? We think this can partly be explained by what we discovered years ago. After meeting Ray, we felt compelled to help him find a publisher for his book, but after contacting a number of Christian publishing houses, we soon learned that they were only looking for books that would sell well—and that meant books considered non-controversial and written by well-known authors with significant platforms. At that point, we prayerfully decided to start our own publishing house. But just the lack of interest that we saw in the publishers was indicative of what was to happen in the church.

Whether we realize it or not, there is tremendous spiritual warfare taking place in our world today. In numerous instances, we are hearing stories of young people going to Christian colleges only to have their spiritual lives shipwrecked. They may have been safer in secular colleges. At the same time, we know of countless numbers of Christians who have no church to go to because the ones that are available have abandoned the simplicity of the Gospel for a universal emerging "spirituality." These believers are now witnessing the apostasy and are looking to ministries like ours for encouragement and help. In many cases, the only encouragement we can offer these people is to assure them that they are not alone in what they see.

As Canadian singer/songwriter Trevor Baker sings in his song "*The Lonely Road*," committed Christians may have to endure much loneliness or isolation in the future for lack of genuine fellowship.

Please remember that while Jesus said we cannot know the day or the hour of His return, He also instructed us to observe the seasons. In saying this, Jesus was sharing a principle that is both profound and very simple:

> Now learn a parable of the fig tree; when his branch is yet tender, and putteth forth leaves, ye know that summer is nigh: So likewise ye, when ye shall see all these things, know that it is near, even at the doors. (Matthew 24: 32-33)

In other words, Jesus was saying that various things must occur before He returns, and when they do occur, we can know that His coming is near. Today, the stage is being set for the fulfillment of the events described in Matthew 24, and in fact, things are moving at a highly accelerated rate. While the church has slept, tares have been sown into God's wheat field (Matthew 13:25). The apostasy we see in the church today is the result of Satan sowing these "tares" in the church.

As we have watched events unfold in the apostate church in recent years, it has been very sobering to see how nearly identical its intents and actions are to that of the New Age movement in moving toward a one-world global order. As you are reading this, religious leaders are shaking hands with political figures in bringing about a *more highly evolved society*. The occultist Alice Bailey, who had much to do with the development of the New Age movement, with all its occult practices and mysticism, predicted that this movement rather than having to move *around* the church would move *through* it. In fact, she saw the church as helping to propel the world into this higher level of consciousness.[2] Sadly, we are hearing almost daily of highly respected Christian leaders with large followings who are now embracing the writings of mystics and contemplative authors. Perhaps they do not realize that the contemplative prayer and mysticism they are passing on to their followers is no different than the occult practices of Alice Bailey with a new "Christianized" twist. And as long as the name of "Jesus" is used, everything is OK, they think.

> Events unfolding in the apostate church are nearly identical to the intents and actions of the New Age movement.

The Fig Tree Ripens

Looking again at the fig tree, we can see that more fruit is developing and getting heavier. Also, as Rick Warren points out (and he himself promotes), we will see a blending of religious, political, and economic forces as future events unfold. Unity will be a key to the future and will be an increasing theme as the world awaits the Antichrist. Considering that we are even now moving toward a one-world order, let us look at our fig tree whose fruit is already there and beginning to get ripe; the events we already see, only to increase, are:

- The unifying of the world's religious thought where eastern-style mystical practice to include Yoga, contemplative prayer, and energy healing practices like Reiki are joining east with west.
- The Purpose Driven P.E.A.C.E. Plan where political, economic, and religious forces are being brought together to form a unified effort.
- Plans for a global currency paving the way to the use of the "mark."
- The accelerating significance of the United Nations leading toward a confederation of nations.
- Increasing interest in the world in finding a Christ figure who can solve the world's economic and political problems and unite the world in peace.
- Increasing moral decay throughout the world to include abortion, violence, pandemic divorce, the dissolution of the family unit, homosexuality, and pedophilia.
- Increasing hatred toward Bible-believing born-again believers.
- The growth of a spirit of antisemitism throughout the world including in much of the organized Christian church today.

- Increased natural disasters to include earthquakes, weather phenomena, and possible volcanic activity.
- Intensifying of wars and rumors of war and man-made disasters.
- Increased skepticism about the Lord's return to include an abandonment of Bible prophecy.
- The appearance of false christs culminating in the appearance of the Antichrist. As a result of mystical practices, to include contemplative prayer, people are already being conditioned to seeing themselves as having a "divine center" where the "Christ" or "I am" resides. Man has become divine.
- An all-out effort to bring the "lost brethren" (evangelicals and Protestants) back into the fold of the Roman Catholic "Mother Church" by the papacy. We are witnessing this more and more today.
- An increasing curiosity and dependence on signs and wonders rather than on the Word of God. Signs and wonders will be seen in the future as the final proof of truth holding sway over many people. This will make it possible for the Antichrist to lead the whole world in a grand delusion as he will be a master at performing signs and wonders.

> Signs and wonders will be seen in the future as the final proof of truth holding sway over many people.

Bridgers and Silencers

Let us pause to look at our fig tree again; I see a couple more figs developing there. One of them is called "the bridgers" and the other is called "the silencers." Unfortunately, both of these figs are growing on the same branch—and the branch has a name on it—it says, "the church." This is odd because these two figs look putrefied, yet they are growing on a branch that looks very healthy.

If you have followed Lighthouse Trails for some time, you may remember a number of years ago a radio interview between LT editor Deborah Dombrowski and radio host Ingrid Schlueter. The title of this broadcast was *Beware the Bridgers: Orthodoxy Is More Than a Doctrinal Statement*.[3] This program talked about the emergence of what one might call a welcoming committee within the church where things God considers foul and unclean are invited in. Oddly enough, it is not the dissenters in the church who are doing this, as would have been the case fifteen or so years ago, but our pastors and Christian leaders—many of whom have had very large followings and been respected as being both conservative and of sound doctrine. But the problem is that these leaders are now gleaning from the writings of New Age, occultic, or mystical authors and quoting them to their followers, oftentimes with a word of recommendation, if not persuasion, to buy these writings and read them in their entirety. We won't take time here to discuss God's view on these things, but if you are curious, you might want to pause to look at Deuteronomy 18:9-14. The question is, why are pastors and respected Christian leaders promoting mystics and occultists? And we use the word "promoting" because this is more than the occasional slip of quoting someone for their clever or witty anecdote. These leaders are both bringing the nail and driving it in. However, in many cases these leaders are obscure as to whether they practice these things themselves; they seem content enough in bringing their followers to the bait, then leaving their followers to fend for themselves. Ingrid Schlueter coined the term "the bridgers" because these leaders in their obscurity seem quite innocent, yet due to their positions of respect and large followings, they are wittingly or unwittingly pulling large numbers of otherwise conservative followers into a trap that these followers would not have ventured to on their own accord. In other words, these bridgers are introducing the more conservative flock to what the Bible calls an abomination.

Then there is the other fig called "the silencers," and it is getting larger. It too looks putrefied, though it is on a healthy looking branch labeled "the church." This fig represents those in the church who regard themselves as having a special corner, an almost elitist attitude, on discernment. While they proclaim their humility, they also pride themselves as having the educational credentials and biblical know-how to steer the church on a straight course. They speak of the embarrassment other ministries are to the body of Christ who are not deemed worthy to hold the compass. A case in point was brought to our attention when two Calvinist men stood before an audience and proceeded to praise each other as the purveyors of sound wisdom, discernment, and biblical scholarship. Then, in turn, they engaged in a joint attack of verbally punching down those they deemed unworthy of discerning the things of God. This ganged venture began when one of them made reference to "housewives and home-school moms" who have no business interfering in things they know nothing about. One referred to such women as "discernment divas" saying that their "greatest ability for [discernment] is not some rational understanding of doctrinal truths but an ability to use a really sharp tongue." Both men on the stage maintained that such things belong to men of wisdom, like themselves. By the way, one of the men is the "right-hand man" to one of the most popular Christian figures today.[4]

After the program, however, this same man, in realizing that he had put his foot in his mouth—figuratively speaking—proceeded to try to remedy the matter lest there be an influx of home-schooling moms and irate husbands knocking at the door. He attempted to remedy the matter by pointing out that he did not mean *all* home-schooling moms but two in particular—namely Ingrid Schlueter, former host of the Crosstalk radio program and Lighthouse Trails Publishing's Deborah Dombrowski.[5] Hoping to put out the spot fires he started, he referred to these women as discernment divas, then proceeded to provide his own derogatory definition of the term.

A Very Real Spiritual Battle

We must not forget the seriousness or the ramifications of what can happen when someone who is endeavoring to help the Body of Christ is knocked down, verbally or otherwise. Again, we are in a spiritual battle—very real, with its own victories and consequences.

The fact is that the darkness hates the light, and when you bring light where there is darkness, it means exposure. We live in a corrupt world where not even the organized church is willing to have the light shine in the dark corners.

But we at Lighthouse Trails were founded on the principle that there is a growing body of believers who have heard God's heart cry to repentance. It is our belief that repentance is meant to be a part of the Christian life, and as we become aware of our imperfections, we endure rather than resist God's refining process in our lives. When John wrote his letters to the seven churches, he did it with this in mind, but history tells us not all seven of them heeded his letters.

Here at Lighthouse Trails, we have endeavored to blow the trumpet over the years, sounding the call to repentance and to a return to the sound doctrine of the Bible. Many have become annoyed with the repeated blasts of the trumpet. All we can say to this is that the time is short, and we remember the words of Jesus when he said, "I must work the works of him that sent me, while it is day: the night cometh, when no man can work" (John 9:4). We will continue to sound the trumpet for as long as we can while doors of opportunity are still open.

Some will say it is better for Christians to be silent and just let God take care of things. But it is through silence that the church in North America has lost so much ground. Rather than helping the process, silence accelerates the work of the enemy. It was through silence that a man called Hitler was able to come to power and murder millions of innocent people.

Sound the Trumpet in the Midst of Apostasy

Keep praying and do what you can to help sound the trumpet. The enemy forces are advancing; in fact, they are within our ranks.

> I set watchmen over you, saying, Hearken to the sound of the trumpet. But they said, We will not hearken. (Jeremiah 6:17)

> Take heed, brethren, lest there be in any of you an evil heart of unbelief, in departing from the living God. But exhort one another daily, while it is called To day; lest any of you be hardened through the deceitfulness of sin. (Hebrews 3:12-13)

Chapter 4

The Peace of God Versus the P.E.A.C.E. of Man

The subject of peace has been thought about, written about, and passed through the lips of countless people over the centuries. Human history has been racked by violence and unrest since the fall of man, making peace an evasive commodity that has only been known for relatively short periods of time.

We wanted to take a look at peace from a biblical perspective considering that the subject is being increasingly talked about in academic, political, and especially religious circles. Rick Warren, for instance, worked hard to implement and promote his P.E.A.C.E. Plan through his three-legged stool approach of melding the world's religious, economic, and political forces into one. As he points out, just as a stool cannot stand unless it has at least three legs, he believes that we cannot achieve world peace without the blending and unifying of these three forces. The New Age movement also has a P.E.A.C.E. plan, and although the acronym utilizes different terms, the intents and goals are similar to those of the Purpose Driven movement.

A Utopian Kingdom on Earth?

The Bible teaches that we are to, "if it be possible, as much as lieth in you, live peaceably with all men" (Romans 12:18). Paul's choice of words here serves as a kind of hesitation in approaching the subject of peace because he knew in his own life what an evasive commodity peace can be. Paul's mission was to preach the Gospel, but in so doing he recounts the perils he faced to include receiving 39 lashes five times, being beaten with rods three times, and being stoned once (2 Corinthians 11:24-25). But this was no great surprise to Paul because God had said of him, "I will shew him how great things he must suffer for my name's sake" (Acts 9:16). When we read of the lives of the other apostles, we learn that their lives were marked by suffering and hardship too. But the Lord had also prepared them for this in saying, "If they have persecuted me, they will also persecute you" (John 15:20). Jesus even went so far as to describe to Peter what kind of death he would suffer for the sake of the Gospel (John 21:18). Is it any wonder, then, if our lives are marked by hardships, misunderstandings, and hostility?

However, in recalling the lives of the apostles and those who have suffered before us, a very important lesson can be learned here. What is being taught in many of today's "new" Christianity churches is that our task is to build God's kingdom here on Earth and that Jesus will return once we have created a form of Utopia here. Similarly, the Catholic Church believes we will create a Utopia once the whole world unites in a devotion to Mary and the Eucharist; this world-wide devotion to the Eucharist will be their version of the Second Coming of Christ.

But as all of these churches unite in trying to bring their version of peace on Earth, they are sadly mistaken and ignorant of what is clearly presented in Scripture. This ignorance of the Scriptures is really a matter of choice than anything else. Just as Peter was not happy to hear what sort of death he would suffer, the emerging religious leaders of today do not want to believe the bleak picture the Bible portrays of the world before Jesus' return. But while Peter accepted Jesus' words, these new Christianity emerging/progressive leaders have bent and twisted Scripture in such a way as to support this Utopian God's-kingdom-on-earth-now theology.

Unbeknownst to the multitudes who are following these globalistic leaders, these current efforts toward global peace are paving the way for the Antichrist whom the Bible warns will implement a peace plan in the last days. Sadly, many proclaiming Christians today are becoming deluded and conditioned to receive this satanic world leader in much the same way that the churches in Germany were conditioned by antisemitic teachings prior to Hitler's rise to power. And many leaders today are becoming modern-day *John the Baptists* for the Antichrist. In her defining of what she called "the regeneration of the churches,"[1] Occultist Alice Bailey proclaimed:

> The Christian church in its many branches can serve as a St. John the Baptist, as a voice crying in the wilderness, and as a nucleus through which world illumination may be accomplished.[2]

While it is true that some of Bible prophecy can be difficult to understand, just a superficial reading of Matthew 24 or Luke 21 should make it abundantly clear that Jesus will return to a world of violence and chaos, not Utopia. But here again these Scriptures have been twisted or ignored.

As for the Book of Revelation, some current-day Bible teachers believe that the prophecies of the Book of Revelation have already happened (i.e., preterism) (as the Catholic Church teaches) or that these events can be prevented (as the New Age and emerging church teaches) in much the same way that Jonah's warning to the Ninevites was turned around. The sad difference is that while the Ninevites responded with repentance, our world is moving further away from godliness. Furthermore, the Book of Revelation depicts events as they *will* actually happen—not as they *might* or *could* happen—because John saw in a vision the future *as it will be.*

Unheeded Warnings

There is, however, God's call today for repentance. There are Christian believers who have been trying to spread abroad God's appeal for repentance and His warnings about the apostasy that has already come upon us. They have been warning that judgment begins in the house of God and that judgment is upon us now too. As we shall see, judgment on the world has only begun and will intensify in the future like birth-pangs on a woman in labor. Paul said, "For we know that the whole creation groaneth and travaileth in pain together until now" (Romans 8:22).

> Could it be this indifference we are witnessing is part of the worldwide delusion Jesus predicted would sweep the Earth in the end times?

It is rather uncanny how the world, in recent years, has witnessed so many natural disasters in the form of earthquakes, floods, and weather phenomena, while the mainstream news media has done so little to cover these events (except to blame them solely on global warming and climate change).[3] In 2011, in Japan, they had a triple disaster of earthquake, tsunami, and nuclear holocaust with possibly millions seriously exposed to radiation in Japan. While unknown quantities of contaminated water were dumped into the ocean, radiation permeated our atmosphere on a global scale; yet at the time it occurred, the media had little to say about this either, except to almost laughingly dismiss it by saying we are getting less exposure than we get from having an X-ray in the dentist's office. The indifference is unbelievable.

The Peace of God Versus the P.E.A.C.E. of Man

Could it be this indifference we are witnessing is part of the world-wide delusion Jesus predicted would sweep the Earth in the end times? Most North Americans, in particular, are living in denial—unwilling to acknowledge the storm clouds looming on our horizon. Is it because most living today have never witnessed catastrophic nation-wide disaster or our shores being invaded by war? But America and Canada *will* know God's judgment (as will the world); and again the reason why we cannot see it is a matter of choice rather than looking at things realistically.

Of all North Americans, our Christian leaders should be seeing and hearing God's warnings of impending judgment. But instead, they are shaking hands with the Devil and prophesying peace, purpose, and prosperity through unity and "community" to their congregations.

Sadly, our world will not know the lasting peace that our religious leaders are predicting—not until after Jesus Christ returns. Yet, God is offering peace and comfort to his own—to those who hear His Word and follow Him. But this peace is not to be found by pursuing our own dreams and goals but rather in seeking to know what God has planned for our lives. The reality is that much of the anguish we experience in life is when things don't turn out the way we had hoped or expected. By contrast, Jesus' apostles knew the peace of God because rather than living in the denial of the postmodern Christians of today, they abided in Christ (1 John 2:28) and fully embraced the lives that God had for them, even when they knew it could mean martyrdom.

Think again of the plight of Peter. Jesus had told him that he would suffer persecution and die a cruel death, yet we do not see Peter wringing his hands at every bend in the road wondering what horrors may await him around the next corner. Peter's life was not one of denial or of fear, but of resolve; the same man who had denied his Lord three times made it his mission to walk with God no matter where that road took him. Consider the events of Acts chapter 12. King Herod had just had James the brother of John killed by the sword, and when he saw that it pleased the Jews, he had Peter arrested too (Acts 12:2-3). No doubt, Herod's intention was to have Peter executed also; and from the believers, realizing the severity of the situation, "prayer was made without ceasing" (v. 5). Meanwhile, Peter had no expectation that an angel would deliver him that night, yet he could sleep in such a dire situation. Peter had learned to entrust his life to the Lord—combining faith and yielding to the will of God—and his heart was ready for whatever awaited him. As the chapter closes, we learn that with the turn of events, it is King Herod who dies and Peter is free.

A Peace Not of This World

It seems that Peter was always learning lessons in life, and here we can see that he had learned to be at peace in even the most drastic of situations, leaving the outcome in God's hands. In his first epistle, Peter shares this perspective:

> Beloved, think it not strange concerning the fiery trial which is to try you, as though some strange thing happened unto you: But rejoice, inasmuch as ye are partakers of Christ's sufferings; that, when his glory shall be revealed, ye may be glad also with exceeding joy. . . . Wherefore let them that suffer according to the will of God commit the keeping of their souls to him in well doing, as unto a faithful Creator. (1 Peter 4:12,13,19)

Like Paul, Peter had learned to be content in every situation. It is the life available to all Christians who yield to God's will, trusting Him to bring them through every situation. How alien to this way of thinking is the church of today where the expectation is that God will make things go our way—even to the point of achieving global peace and a Utopian society. These are things that Jesus never promised us and, in fact, warned would not happen. While Christian leaders of today are speaking of establishing God's kingdom *on earth* before Jesus returns, Jesus said, "My kingdom is *not of this world*" (John 18:36—emphasis added).

Should we not, as believers in Jesus Christ, be about our Father's business? So while we should try to live at peace with all men, our objective should be to spread the Gospel to all mankind. When Jesus spoke of the kingdom of Heaven, he never used illustrations that support the kingdom-now teachings of today. Rather, He spoke of hidden things and small beginnings. There was the parable of the mustard seed, which has a small and humble beginning yet grows into a tree (Matthew 13:31-32). Then there is the parable of the leaven, which a woman "hid" in three measures of meal, yet it leavened the whole lump of dough (Matthew 13:33). We used to wonder what Jesus meant by these parables, but over the last several years we have become aware that while the apostate church has been very visible and trumpeting their attempts to bring about a world-wide "reformation," and revival, simultaneously an unseen body of believers all over the world has been returning to their first love and walking in an attitude of brokenness and a contrite heart:

> The sacrifices of God are a broken spirit: a broken and a contrite heart, O God, thou wilt not despise. (Psalm 51:17)

I am sure it is this body of believers that Jesus refers to as the kingdom of Heaven—not the boisterous liberal body who will sacrifice the Gospel in their pursuit of peace.

Pursuing Peace But Not God

Peace is one of those unusual commodities (though very valuable), which cannot be achieved through direct pursuit. When nations have walked in repentance and pursued righteousness, God has blessed them with peace. But when nations have become vile and unruly and exchange the pursuit for God for a pursuit of things, the aspiration for peace remains out of reach.

The kingdom of Heaven is less visible in its pursuits because its goals are different than the earthly ones of the apostate church. Our commission is to spread the Gospel, and it is to this cause that we need to be faithful. The kingdom of Heaven is less visible in another way too—it is something that works in the hearts of people bringing about change through repentance and godliness. Compare this with Rick Warren's "new reformation," which is based, by Warren's own admission, by deeds rather than creeds.[4] All are invited to this reformation, regardless of what anyone believes. But Jesus put it plainly when He said that a man's actions, be they good or evil, proceed from what is in the heart. A reformation based on action that does not deal with the heart is futile indeed. In order to change our world into a better place, hearts would need to change. The only way our nation could have a turn-around at this point would be through a widespread turning to the Lord in humility and repentance, but how can this happen when even the church is not walking as it should today?

> Righteousness exalteth a nation: but sin is a reproach to any people. (Proverbs 14:34)

Today, we often hear many Christian groups quoting 2 Chronicles 7:14: "If my people, which are called by my name, shall humble themselves, and pray . . . then will I hear from heaven . . . and will heal their land." But there is a part of this Scripture that is usually ignored: "If my people, which are called by my name, shall humble themselves, and pray, and seek my face, *and turn from their wicked ways*; then will I hear from heaven, and *will forgive their sin*, and will heal their land" (emphasis added)

All the prayers for America by apostate leaders are in vain because these leaders (and their followers) have not even repented themselves. On the contrary, they continue to promote and exalt a kingdom-now, dominionist, mystical, experiential "gospel." Just look how popular books like *The Shack* and *The Purpose Driven Life* have been with new ones like these on the horizon every day. These books make people feel good about themselves, but they do not bring the heart to repentance.

Unfortunately, the peace that our world desires will not be known because its pursuits are ungodly. For the true believer, however, peace is an achievable commodity. Jesus promised His disciples peace when He said:

> Peace I leave with you, my peace I give unto you: *not as the world* giveth, give I unto you. Let not your *heart* be troubled, neither let it be afraid. (John 14:27—emphasis added)

Notice that Jesus says two things here: First, the peace He gives is not like the peace the world gives. In other words, don't pursue peace from the world. Secondly, Jesus speaks of the heart. Peace, for the Christian, is a matter of the heart. And, as I alluded to before, Christians with false expectations (who are living in denial) will be disappointed again and again and live lives of anguish. The Bible says that "fear hath torment" (1 John 4:18). But the disciples faced their fears; they acknowledged the fact that they would encounter persecution and hardships, then they entrusted their lives to God as unto a faithful Creator. After all, the God who made us is also able to take care of us. And He has promised to abide in us (1 John 3:24) if we abide in Him.

> **The peace He gives is not like the peace the world gives. In other words, don't pursue peace from the world.**

Even though we cannot and will not know the day or the hour of Jesus' return, Jesus did instruct us to observe the seasons. Right now, we are at that place Jeremiah speaks of where he says,

> They have healed also the hurt of the daughter of my people slightly, saying, Peace, peace; when there is no peace. (Jeremiah 6:14)

In a time when pastors should be leading their churches in repentance and evangelists calling our nation back to righteousness, we have peace plans underway. The future of our nation and our world is bleak, so we should not be offering false assurances that will only be dashed to the ground.

The Bible offers peace for the true believer, but it is a peace that transcends what the world has to offer. Looking to the world for peace will only lead to disappointment. The peace God gives is of the heart, and it does not depend on our circumstances. It results from looking reality in the face but then looking to God and keeping our eyes on Him—trusting Him to deliver us and keep us under the shadow of His wings.

> Open ye the gates, that the righteous nation which keepeth the truth may enter in. Thou wilt keep him in perfect peace, whose mind is stayed on thee: because he trusteth in thee. Trust ye in the LORD for ever: for in the LORD JEHOVAH is everlasting strength. (Isaiah 26:2-4)

Part II

A Faith Worth Protecting

Chapter 5

Signs & Wonders! Five Things You Should Consider

I. Setting Things Up With Great Delusion

Jesus taught his disciples that in the last days, a time of mass delusion will come upon the Earth. He said:

> For false Christs and false prophets shall rise, and shall shew *signs and wonders*, to seduce, if it were possible, even the elect. But take ye heed: behold, I have foretold you all things. (Mark 13:22-23; emphasis added)

Likewise, Paul spoke of this time when he said:

> Now the Spirit speaketh expressly, that in the latter times some shall depart from the faith, giving heed to seducing spirits, and doctrines of devils. (1 Timothy 4:1)

If we look at what is happening in the world today, the only logical conclusion is that we have already entered into that period of history. The world is going through a mystical paradigm shift where an increasingly high number of people are engaging in occultic mystical practices which are leading them into a New Age all-paths-lead-to-God kind of mentality.

This is not only happening in the world, but it is happening in the church as well. It is shocking to see that doctrines and values formerly held sacred are now being discarded. Many Christian leaders today have replaced the reading and study of Scripture with having spiritual experiences or what Jesus referred to above as *signs and wonders*. In effect, multitudes of Christians are being led to believe that if they can have some type of spiritual experience or witness a miracle, that will bear more validity than the words of Scripture itself.

What we have now generated is a delusion so great that if one has an "experience" that contradicts the Bible, one will hold the experience as valid and not the Bible because the experience is seen as tangible and therefore more real. But this is an insult to our God because as David points out in a Psalm:

> I will worship toward thy holy temple, and praise thy name for thy lovingkindness and for thy truth: for *thou hast magnified thy word above all thy name*. (Psalm 138:2; emphasis added)

God holds His Word in highest esteem as being entirely truthful, but many would rather trust and rely on their own experiences as their standard for truth.

We have become like the masses in former centuries who believed that the world is flat (because it appears to be flat), while the Bible itself refers to it as a globe (Isaiah 40:22). Frankly, in a practical day-to-day sense, it makes no difference to me whether the Earth be flat or round, except perhaps a fear of falling off the edge if I went too far, but when it comes to spiritual matters, the truth is essential as to where I will be spending eternity. You see, we have an advocate with the Father—Jesus Christ Himself, who is all Truth and paid the price to take us to Heaven; but we also have a deceiver, Satan, who is the father of lies and is intent on leading us to Hell.

It is imperative to realize that not all paths lead to Heaven, or should I say, there is only one path to God, and Jesus is that Path (John 14:6). All the other paths of the world believe that man is intrinsically good and can therefore earn his way to Heaven. Only the Gospel reveals the truth that we were born sinners, and our transgressions have alienated us from God; but Jesus paid the price for our sins, and through His death and resurrection we have, by faith, salvation (having been forgiven), righteousness (imputed and not earned), peace with God, and the grace for holy living (being "raised with Christ").

Nothing could make the enemy of our souls happier than to steal away our soul, and his primary way of doing this is through deception because Satan is a master of lies.

II. Are All Signs and Wonders From the Same Source?

Knowing that we are in a time of great delusion, let us focus here on one aspect of it, where Jesus referred to it in Mark 13 as the realm of signs and wonders.

In doing a Scripture search on the words "signs" and "wonders" appearing together, I expected to find only a few references but was surprised to find eighteen references in the Old Testament and fourteen references in the New Testament. The majority of these references in both the Old and New Testaments were used in a positive sense. In the Old Testament, the most common examples were those referring to how Moses delivered the Israelites through signs and wonders, while in the New Testament, the most common examples were those of God confirming the preaching of the Gospel by the apostles through signs and wonders. When used in a negative sense, the words "signs" and "wonders" were usually used together in a prophetic warning to avoid false leaders and prophets.

Now, the point I wish to make here is that we cannot make a sweeping statement saying that all signs and wonders are bad, nor can we say that they are all good; rather we need to look beyond the physical manifestations and determine the source from which they come. But in the cases of Moses and the apostles, God was confirming the ministry and message of these men. Too often, however, signs and wonders are unquestioningly accepted as being "from God."

As a former Catholic, I can remember stories from my youth and up of miraculous signs taken as divine confirmation that God has spoken, be it the apparitions of Mary giving messages that contradict Scripture or of communion wafers that bleed or pulse contradicting the message of the Gospel (Jesus clearly said that the "flesh profiteth nothing" (John 6:63) and the book of Hebrews speaks of a sacrifice made once for all time—Hebrews 9:27-28;10:10,12,14). In the case of the Catholic Church, there are strange manifestations that inevitably glorify man, and those who perform such wonders bear a message that requires redemption through human performance as opposed to grace by faith alone. It is not always easy at the surface level to recognize the meaning behind a sign or wonder, but we do have the Holy Spirit and the Word of God as witnesses for us.

A key passage from the Old Testament that strictly forbids the unquestioning acceptance of all signs and wonders is the following:

> If there arise among you a prophet, or a dreamer of dreams, and giveth thee a sign or a wonder, *and the sign or the wonder come to pass,* whereof he spake unto thee, saying, Let us go after other gods, which thou hast not known, and let us serve them; Thou shalt not hearken unto the words of that prophet, or that dreamer of dreams: *for the LORD your God proveth you,* to know whether ye love the LORD your God with all your heart and with all your soul. Ye shall walk after the LORD your God, and fear him, and keep his commandments, and obey his voice, and ye shall serve him, and cleave unto him. (Deuteronomy 13:1-4; emphasis added)

Notice how explicit these instructions are about maintaining a faithful and unwavering devotion to the Lord *even when* the sign or wonder has "come to pass!" It is never enough that a sign or wonder happens; it must always be tested as to whether or not it supports and confirms God's Word.

Yet, for many people today (including many Christians), if a strange, paranormal manifestation occurs, that is evidence enough that it must be from God without any recognition or acknowledgment that dark supernatural forces can do these things. For example, the manifestations of holy laughter, "slaying in the Spirit," jerkings, convulsions, twisting, contortions, and animal-like behaviors have all been witnessed under the "ministering" of eastern gurus who draw on Kundalini energy (serpent power) to do their work. And, as discerning believers, when we listen to the doctrine or teaching of these ministers (who are so wrapped up in manifestations that they hardly preach at all), we can only conclude that these are wolves in sheep's clothing deceiving and being deceived. Many of the ministers actually even mock the preaching of God's Word and arrogantly proclaim or imply that because they have the power to do these things, they are greater than all preachers. But God has chosen to use the "foolishness of preaching to save them that believe" (1 Corinthians 1:21).

Now, I'm not saying that these ministers necessarily know they are wolves. For the most part, they believe they are doing God a service. But as Jesus pointed out, many ministers are just hirelings in that they "careth not for the sheep" (John 10:13); they will fleece the flock for gain, but they will not lay down their lives for the sheep. Jesus said, "I lay down my life for the sheep" (John 10:15).

III. Preparing the Way ... But For "Who"?

Unbeknownst to themselves, many of today's ministers are paving the way for the Antichrist. They are like John the Baptists for the Antichrist as their efforts are actually preparing the hearts of the people for such a leader. This is especially true of ministers who minimize the preaching of sound doctrine and maximize on manifestations "from God." I say this because the Antichrist will be a master of signs and wonders, which will actually be his trademark and likely the primary way he will get the world to believe in him. In speaking of the coming Antichrist, Paul had this to say:

> And then shall that Wicked be revealed, whom the Lord shall consume with the spirit of his mouth, and shall destroy with the brightness of his coming: Even him, whose coming is after the working of Satan with all power and signs and lying wonders, And with all deceivableness of unrighteousness in them that perish; because they received not the love of the truth, that they might be saved. (2 Thessalonians 2:8-10)

Meanwhile, people's hearts are being conditioned for this figure who will integrate the economic, political, and religious sectors together under a world-wide peace plan while confirming his authority and power through lying wonders. It will be a "grand day" for the world as millions will be duped by a man with a charismatic mantle and anointing like unto Adolf Hitler who stirred up a nation; but this time it will be the whole world. In fact, there are many similarities today between our country (the USA) and much of the world with that of the mindset of much of society in Germany prior to Hitler coming into power: In both cases, we see an emergence of antisemitism, even among those claiming to be Christians; churches and Bible colleges are becoming more and more liberal and humanistic in theology and rule; spiritual apostasy can be seen everywhere; and political powers are bringing about radical changes to the infrastructure of our society. At Lighthouse Trails, as we watch the pace of things accelerating, we often wonder if we may have less time than we think.

This is a time in history when it is imperative for Christian believers to stay alert and warn all we can about the delusion coming upon the world and the apostasy taking place in the church. The future will unfold as predicted in the Bible, but we can be prepared and help prepare others for whatever comes.

IV. Signs and Wonders—and a True Minister of God

As for the signs and wonders delusion, it is important to remember that if someone performs a sign or a wonder, he is operating beyond the realm of his own strength and mere physical laws, but we cannot automatically assume he is operating from God just as we cannot assume he is operating from the demonic realm. To help us discern, we can apply the test of 1 John 4:1-3 and ask ourselves what is the *message* of the person performing the wonder? Is he glorifying God and promoting the Gospel, or is he glorifying himself as if he were greater than all other ministers? The mark of a true minister of God is humility and not pride. Jesus said of the true John the Baptist, "Among those that are born of women there is not a greater prophet than John the Baptist" (Luke 7:28). Here is a man who was anointed of the Holy Spirit while still in his mother's womb (Luke 1:15, 41). Yet, we also read in John 10:41 that "John [the Baptist] did no miracle." John was a unique individual, and we need more like him. When he said of Jesus, "this my joy therefore is fulfilled. He must increase, but I must decrease" (John 3:29-30), in a few words, John indicated his attributes. He was a humble man with the right priorities who remained obedient to his mission. He did not need to do a sign or a wonder because he revealed Jesus and had prepared the way for Him.

V. The Purpose of Signs and Wonders

Signs and wonders are performed for a purpose. In the Old Testament, they were performed to deliver God's people:

> Which hast set signs and wonders in the land of Egypt, even unto this day, and in Israel, and among other men. . . . And hast brought forth thy people Israel out of the land of Egypt with signs, and with wonders. (Jeremiah 32:20-21)

In the New Testament, Jesus performed signs and wonders to show He was approved of and from God. Peter spoke of this on the day of Pentecost:

> Jesus of Nazareth, a man approved of God among you by miracles and wonders and signs. (Acts 2:22)

The apostles likewise did signs and wonders:

> And fear came upon every soul: and many wonders and signs were done by the apostles. (Acts 2:43)

The book of Hebrews makes it clear that these signs and wonders were done to confirm the Gospel message:

> How shall we escape, if we neglect so great salvation [the Gospel message]; which at the first began to be spoken by the Lord, and was confirmed unto us by them that heard him; God also bearing them witness, both with signs and wonders, and with divers miracles, and gifts of the Holy Ghost, according to his own will? (Hebrews 2:3-4)

Yet, we know that Jesus rebuked the seeking of signs and wonders where the Gospel is not received and believed:

> Except ye see signs and wonders, ye will not believe. (John 4:48)

> An evil and adulterous generation seeketh after a sign. (Matthew 12:39)

And this is the way it is today. People flock to witness manifestations, but they will not flock to hear the Gospel—to hear about sin and judgment and faith in the finished work of Christ on the Cross. The fact is, we do not need to be seeking signs and wonders because that is not where the real power lies. The prophet Elijah, a man who called fire down from Heaven to burn his sacrifice, subsequently had an encounter with God while hiding in a cave. As the Lord passed by, He sent powerful manifestations: first, in a strong wind that "rent the mountains, and brake in pieces the rocks before the Lord" (1 Kings 19:11); second, there was an earthquake; and third, there was a fire. Yet, it says that the Lord was not in any of these, and Elijah remained unmoved from his fear and despair. But, after the fire, there was "a still small voice" (v. 12) and then we read,

> And it was so, when Elijah heard it, that he wrapped his face in his mantle, and went out, and stood in the entering in of the cave. (v. 13)

The point is really quite simple. While God can demonstrate His power in marvelous and supernatural ways, it was the word of the Lord that brought Elijah out of the cave, encouraged him, instructed him, and sent him on his way. And this is the problem with signs and wonders that are not accompanied by and supported by God's Word; nothing really changes of lasting value. People may witness signs and wonders, but that is not going to bring personal transformation or eternal salvation to them. Only when a life has been surrendered to the Lord through faith in hearing the Gospel do we have changes that are of a true and lasting spiritual value. We know that the apostles went out to preach the Gospel, and signs and wonders followed them—the emphasis being on the Gospel. Paul made it clear in his letters that the power that changes lives for eternity is in the Gospel. It is the power to save:

> For the preaching of the cross is to them that perish foolishness; but unto us which are saved it is the power of God. (1 Corinthians 1:18)

> For I am not ashamed of the gospel of Christ: for it is the power of God unto salvation to every one that believeth; to the Jew first, and also to the Greek. (Romans 1:16)

I know there are people reading this who have great needs and are hoping for a word of encouragement to get through a particular situation. And there always will be needs of one sort or another where at times it seems it would take a miracle to get through the present

---

"It Must Be From God!"

Some are tempted to think that if the manifestations they are observing are magnificent enough, it *must* be from God. Yet, the Antichrist who is coming will do signs and wonders far beyond the scope of what we are seeing today—to the extent that the whole world will be deceived. What we should be looking at is the doctrine of these individuals and ask ourselves if it fully lines up and agrees with the pure and simple Gospel handed down to us in Scripture. So often, you will find it does not—if the Gospel is even being preached at all![1]

—Roger Oakland

challenge. If you feel this way, let me say this: God is faithful, and He is there for those who hope in His mercy (Psalm 147:11). But as Christians, let us be careful not to be caught up in fear and worry that would rob us of our effectiveness for God and of the abundant life God has for us. Jesus said:

> The thief cometh not, but for to steal, and to kill, and to destroy: I am come that they might have life, and that they might have it more abundantly. (John 10:10)

Remember also that Jesus said:

> But seek ye first the kingdom of God, and his righteousness; and all these things [our needs] shall be added unto you. (Matthew 6:33)

God is faithful, and He *can* be depended upon to deliver us in whatever trials we face. Peter writes in his epistle:

> Wherefore let them that suffer according to the will of God commit the keeping of their souls to him in well doing, as unto a faithful Creator. (1 Peter 4:19)

We are on a journey through life, and there are many obstacles along the path that would slow us down and rob us of our attention to the things of the Lord. Let us not lose sight of our destination.

Chapter 6

Drugs, Meditation, & "A Fully Developed Spirituality"

Lessons From A Former Shaman For Today's Church

It is interesting how God orchestrates things in life which demonstrate His great love and ongoing mercy to ordinary people like myself. More specifically, I am thinking right now about how years ago I happened to come across a copy of a nearly forgotten book at the university library while working on a project. I still find it amazing that this secular humanistic library even had a copy of *Stories From Indian Wigwams and Northern Campfires*—a book written by a missionary to the Canadian Native peoples of the 1800s sharing not only his life among them but the incredible stories they would tell him as they would warm themselves before a fire. This book is a treasure of the long-forgotten heritage of the Cree and Saulteaux tribes and how their lives were wonderfully transformed through the proclamation of the Gospel.

Though I first read that book over thirty-five years ago as a young university student, in 2010 God put it on our hearts at Lighthouse Trails to publish this book; then, when we were preparing to release it for publication, Nanci Des Gerlaise, a Christian Canadian Cree, contacted us about a book she had written titled *Muddy Waters*. The great surprise was that Nanci, to whom we then sent a review copy of the *Wigwam* manuscript, recognized in it the name Mask-e-pe-toon as being the name of the best friend of her great, great grandfather. Nanci then agreed to write the foreword to our edition of the *Wigwam* book. We also agreed to publish *Muddy Waters*.

"The Foolishness of God"

Sometime after publishing the *Wigwam* book and *Muddy Waters*, we added a DVD film titled *I'll Never Go Back!: The Testimony of Chief Shoefoot* (which can also be seen freely on YouTube). In this documentary, Chief Shoefoot shares his own story of what life has been like for him both before and after he received the Gospel—hence his words "I'll never go back." Chief Shoefoot is a member of the native people known as the Yanomamo. The Yanomamo reside in a northern region of South America bordering Venezuela and Brazil. Hearing that Chief Shoefoot is part of a Yanomamo tribe especially caught my interest because I remembered studying these people in an anthropology class at the university.

Anthropologists have been studying the Yanomamo for many years now, and the typical reaction by many secular anthropologists to missionary outreaches to these people is that the Yanomamo people would have been better off if they had been left alone. Granted various missionary efforts were probably not conducted as they should have been, the fact remains that Jesus commissioned the Gospel to be shared with the whole world. What makes this video unique is that it is the testimony of an actual member of the Yanomamo tribe sharing his viewpoint and his side of the story; and his conclusion is an emphatic *yes* to having received the Gospel. Contrary to what these anthropologists are saying, Chief Shoefoot makes it clear that his life has been forever changed for the better.

Drugs, Meditation & "A Fully Developed Spirituality"

In today's current "progressive" emergent/woke atmosphere, much of the Christian mission field has been marred by the mentality that we should be less intrusive about sharing the Gospel (as Roger Oakland defines in his booklet, *New Missiology: Doing Missions Without the Gospel*). Now don't get me wrong; it's true there may be many non-spiritual aspects of a culture that don't need to be changed, but the Gospel is very intrusive in calling all people everywhere to repent (change direction, acknowledging one's sinful condition), to believe on the Lord Jesus Christ (His sacrifice on the Cross and His resurrection), and to put their trust solely in Him for salvation. Jesus came as Savior to the whole world, and all people from all tribes and nations are offered one way to God. But today numerous mission organizations have been taking a more "politically correct" approach in assuming that every culture already has within its religious traditions an acceptable pathway to God, and our only duty is to encourage the people of these other cultures in what they already believe and are already doing with little more than perhaps an occasional reference to the Jesus Christ of the Bible.[1] The sad truth and reality is that although many peoples and cultures may believe in some type of supreme being and do have a sense of right and wrong (instilled into man through our God-given conscience), the Gospel is unique. It is God's revealed Word and offer of salvation based on grace through faith alone as opposed to a gospel of good works based on a belief in the innate goodness of mankind and God's willingness to accept any and all man-made plans of salvation.

The truth is that God has declared in his Word that all are sinners and in need of a Savior. So while it may be true that God has not called us to impose European or Western customs on the indigenous peoples of the world, the Gospel is God's "culture" for all mankind in that it calls all people to repentance and faith in Jesus Christ. All I can say is that I personally am so glad that

God "imposed" Himself on me when I received Christ as my Savior; and in both *Muddy Waters* and *I'll Never Go Back* lie the powerful and convincing testimony of two people—a medicine man's daughter (in the book) and a former shaman or witchdoctor (in the film). Their stories are evidence that knowing Jesus Christ as Savior is more precious than anything the world has to offer and does beseech us to forsake those things displeasing to Him.

Albeit, God has given all people everywhere a conscience—a sense of right and wrong—it remains that the spirituality of all tribes and nations must give way to the truth of the Gospel rather than trying to reshape the Gospel to make it more palatable to any particular culture. After all, what part of the Gospel would we change? The fact is, the "preaching of the cross is to them that perish foolishness; but unto us which are saved it is the power of God" (1 Corinthians 1:18). Thus, it remains that the Gospel will always be offensive and politically incorrect to the unbeliever regardless of cultural setting. The Gospel is offensive not because it is the "white man's religion" (which it never was) but because it is the way God chose to redeem mankind—which appears foolish to the carnal mind. But as Scripture declares, "the foolishness of God is wiser than men; and the weakness of God is stronger than men" (1 Corinthians 1:25).

A Fully Developed "Spirituality"

In *I'll Never Go Back,* Chief Shoefoot shares about how he became a shaman (i.e., witchdoctor) and the spirituality that ensued. In watching his testimony, I was amazed by the realization that as he was describing his spirituality as a shaman, he was describing the very spirituality being promoted in the church today as "cutting-edge Christianity." In fact, Chief Shoefoot's spirituality was far *ahead* of the current contemplative prayer movement and the New Age of today. Furthermore, his people were already incorporating spiritual disciplines into

Drugs, Meditation & "A Fully Developed Spirituality"

their meditative practices. When I realized this, I listened to Chief Shoefoot very attentively and with much interest because I understood then that they had been practicing "contemplative spirituality"* and the "spiritual disciplines" probably for many centuries—perhaps even longer than the Desert Fathers** (after all, the meditation the Desert Fathers practiced didn't originate with them but rather was most likely "borrowed" from the east.[2]) In listening to Chief Shoefoot describe his spirituality as a shaman, I also realized he was, at the same time, describing where the spirituality of contemplative prayer, the New Age, and the spiritual disciplines will be in the future.

So, while the meditative practices and disciplines of the Desert Fathers phased out to near extinction after the Middle Ages then were later resurrected by Catholic monks such as Thomas Merton and Basil Pennington, the Yanomamo have preserved and developed these practices and brought them to full fruition. In other words, as the church and the New Age movement are in unison developing these practices, they will in time become like the Yanomamo. Let me explain.

In the film, Chief Shoefoot describes how he was introduced to shamanism at an early age because he was far advanced for his age in spiritual acuteness, he was told. Like contemplative prayer and New Age meditation, connection with "God" is accomplished by going into an altered state of consciousness (i.e., the silence). In

---

* Contemplative Spirituality: A belief system that uses ancient mystical practices to induce altered states of consciousness (the silence) and is rooted in mysticism and the occult but often wrapped in Christian terminology. The premise of contemplative spirituality is pantheistic (God is all) and panentheistic (God is in all). Common terms used for this movement are "spiritual formation," "the silence," "the stillness," "ancient-wisdom," "spiritual disciplines," and many others. ** The Desert Fathers were Catholic monks and hermits in the early Middle Ages who lived in the wilderness and practiced various mystical rituals.

the case of the Yanomamo, a drug is used for this purpose along with chanting (mantra), rhythm, and dancing. Spiritual disciplines (to include the withholding of food [i.e., fasting] and sleep) are also used to make the spiritual senses more acute. As I listened to Chief Shoefoot describe his story, I could see he was much more advanced than the mystics and contemplative prayer leaders of today. He literally saw into the spirit world and beheld various spirits for which the Yanomamo even had names.

The Yanomamo shaman recognizes the spirit world as a reality, not a superstition. According to Chief Shoefoot, spirits of various sorts are seen as desirable and are invited to "get inside your chest" while others are avoided as being evil. I am reminded how contemplative pioneer Richard Foster warns his students to beware of dangerous spirits when they practice contemplative prayer. In *Faith Undone,* Roger Oakland talks about this:

> Proponents of contemplative prayer say the purpose of contemplative prayer is to tune in with God and hear His voice. However, Richard Foster claims that practitioners must use caution. He admits that in contemplative prayer "we are entering deeply into the spiritual realm" and that sometimes it is not the realm of God even though it is "supernatural." He admits there are spiritual beings and that a prayer of protection should be said beforehand something to the effect of "All dark and evil spirits must now leave."[3]

What Chief Shoefoot realized too late is that *none* of these spirits are good, and those considered to be evil cannot be avoided either. He learned that once a person enters into the occultic or contemplative realm, he becomes subject to the spirits that inhabit that realm. Christian mystics who engage in contemplative prayer think they are encountering the Holy Spirit, but Chief Shoefoot literally saw that this realm is inhabited by nothing more than demons who in time also made their habitation in him (and in other members of the tribe).

With this in mind, it is understandable that much of the activity of the tribe was marked by immorality and violence. Even anthropologists who are unsympathetic to the Christianizing of these tribes recognize a problem in their social and domestic interactions. Consider, for example, the following quote from an anthropological source regarding the role and treatment of wives in Yanomamo culture:

> It is interesting to watch the behavior of women when their husbands return from a hunting trip or a visit. The men march slowly across the village and retire silently into their hammocks. The woman, no matter what she is doing, hurries home and quietly but rapidly prepares a meal for her husband. Should the wife be slow at doing this, the husband is within his rights to beat her. Most reprimands meted out by irate husbands take the form of blows with the hand or with a piece of firewood, but a good many husbands are even more severe. Some of them chop their wives with the sharp edge of a machete or ax, or shoot them with a barbed arrow in some nonvital area, such as in the buttocks or leg. Many men are given to punishing their wives by holding the hot end of a glowing stick against them, resulting in serious burns. . . . It is not uncommon for a man to injure his errant wife seriously; and some men have even killed wives. Women expect this kind of treatment. Those who are not too severely treated might even measure their husband's concern in terms of the frequency of minor beatings they sustain. I overheard two young women discussing each other's scalp scars. One of them commented that the other's husband must really care for her since he has beaten her on the head so frequently! . . . Some men . . . seem to think that it is reasonable to beat their wife once in a while "just to keep them on their toes."[4]

For lack of space, let me just say that the interactions of men with each other both within and between tribes is often not peaceable either. But, in any case, Native Spirituality* plays a highly significant role in the happenings of these tribes.

Now, I imagine my statement made earlier—that those who practice "Christian" contemplative prayer or New Age mysticism will eventually become like the Yanomamo—must sound too extreme or at least a tongue-in-cheek statement. Actually, given the popularity today of mystical meditative practices, it would bring me much comfort if I were to know I am completely wrong in this assertion. But I am deeply concerned about people, many of whom are Christians, who are delving into contemplative prayer, eastern meditative practices, Yoga, Reiki, and New Age mysticism thinking they will better themselves (and come into a more enlightened consciousness) by doing so. All of these are occult practices that will tie the user in with the demonic realm though he may think he is connecting with "good" spirits, spirit guides, or the Holy Spirit.

Seeing that mystical meditation has become such common place, I realize a very great number of people would also see the statement I just made as fanatical or as a conspiracy theory. But the fact is, a conspiracy is already underway, instigated by Satan himself and performed by his vast number of demons. As Ray Yungen suggests in his book *A Time of Departing*, mysticism will have much to do with the great delusion that is already sweeping throughout the world. He points out that a mystical sector or element inhabits the various religions of the world, so it would only make sense that if the religions of the world are to unite, mysticism will play a major role.

It is not unusual for people to join the New Age movement or engage in Yoga or meditative practices like contemplative prayer in order to reap health benefits, to include higher levels of relaxation,

---

* To understand the structure and complexities of Native Spirituality, read *Muddy Waters* by Canadian Cree author, Nanci Des Gerlaise.

Drugs, Meditation & "A Fully Developed Spirituality"

or to live a more victorious life, but all the while, they are being introduced to something demonic both in origin and operation. The Bible makes a clear statement about occult or mystical practices in Deuteronomy 18:9-12 by sounding the alarm that these practices are "an abomination unto the LORD." Then, too, Jesus warned against praying as the heathen do by using "vain repetitions" (Matthew 6:7), which is a clear indictment against chanting or the mantra-like words and phrases used in contemplative or meditative prayer.

The only real difference between the mysticism or Native Spirituality of the Yanomamo and the "Christian mystic" of today is that the Yanomamo have a *fully developed spirituality* and are far ahead of the mystical leaders and contemplative prayer proponents of the present. An example of this is that the Yanomamo have developed a broader variety of techniques that enable them to enter "the silence" more quickly. For instance, a drug is used that quickly brings the participant into an altered state of consciousness.

A Deadly Direction

Now, because the Yanomamo have been practicing mysticism and the spiritual disciplines for a very long time, it stands to reason that what they have brought to fruition will, in time, be the outcome of these practices that are sweeping through our churches today. So, without attempting or pretending to be prophetic, we can forecast the outcome of these practices based on where they have brought the Yanomamo and other peoples who practice Native Spirituality. The reason why I can say these things is because when the Yanomamo shaman engages in mysticism, he enters the same mystical realm that Christians do when they engage in contemplative prayer. In both cases, they enter into an occultic realm and put themselves at the mercy of the demons who inhabit those realms. Unfortunately, the demons are not merciful but rather pose as angels of light or the Holy Spirit and lead the practitioner away from the simple truth of the Gospel. While promising much, they deliver what is ultimately harmful to the practitioner. Currently, contemplative or mystical prayer is sweeping the church with the sales pitch that it enhances physical, mental, and spiritual well being to include relaxation and a direct connection to hearing from God. But as we have been attempting to demonstrate over the past two decades with our research materials, contemplative prayer and mysticism do indeed connect one with a spiritual realm, but that realm is not God, and it is not good.

And while the New Age movement promises an Age of Aquarius (or enlightenment) as an age of peace and oneness if we all engage in mystical prayer, the Bible indicates that the last days will be marked by unrest and war. And if we look at the Yanomamo, who have been practicing spirituality for centuries, we can see that the lives of these tribesmen and women are marked not by peace but by unrest and violence. If all that the mystics are saying were true, you would think that when the anthropologists discovered the Yanomamo peoples they would have discovered Utopian bliss and celestial innocence; but rather, violence and unrest were discovered. The Yanomamo have tried and proven that *spirituality* is not what sustains a people, but as Chief Shoefoot points out after his conversion, our hope is in Jesus Christ alone. It is tragically ironic that while a Yanomamo chief, like Chief Shoefoot, has time tested and proven that mysticism does not work and has now turned to Jesus, countless Christians are now turning to mysticism (the very thing that Chief Shoefoot renounced) to find answers.

Babylon

Interestingly enough, the Book of Revelation makes reference to the re-emergence in the last days of "that great city Babylon" (Revelation 18:21) which was in ancient times a center of idolatry and mysticism but in the end times will be the mercantile hub of false religion. Revelation 18 describes Babylon as "the habitation of devils, and the hold of every foul spirit, and a cage of every unclean and hateful bird" (Revelation 18:2). But how can it be that a city that practices contemplative prayer and mysticism can be frowned upon by God to such a degree? Is it not because the mystical or occultic realm is the habitation of devils? Chief Shoefoot says it is so. Of further significance is verse 23 that states, "for thy merchants were the great men of the earth; for by thy sorceries were all nations deceived" (Revelation 18:23). If we consult *Strong's Concordance,* we find that the Greek word used for "sorceries" is *pharmakeia* (pharmacy) signifying medication and derived from the word *pharmakon* signifying drugs (i.e., spell-giving potions). It seems very possible, therefore, that the mystics of the last days will incorporate drug use into their mystical practices, and as indicated in verse 23 above, this may become a great merchandising endeavor where people all over the world will be using mind-altering drugs.

The Catholic mystic Thomas Merton, who helped to pave the way for contemplative prayer to enter our generation, said he felt sorry for the hippies of the '60s who used LSD because, as he pointed out, they could have achieved the same result by practicing contemplative prayer.[5] But the mystic of the end times may actually feel sorry for Thomas Merton because drug use could make the mystical state much more readily attainable to anyone. Contemplative prayer takes some effort by incorporating a mantra-like word or phrase to create a hypnotic state whereas, in the future, the same result could be achieved by popping a pill or inhaling the smoke of a drug (such as marijuana)—hence "instant" spirituality! Yet, all the while God's statement about such practices will be, "for by thy sorceries were all nations deceived." Apparently, whatever happens will be a massive global effort, and by it, people all over the world will be living in great delusion.*

---

*Read Richard and Linda Nathan's booklet *The Cross and the Marijuana Leaf* regarding marijuana, a drug which is fast becoming legalized for recreational use throughout the U.S. Also read their fascinating booklet, *Psychedelic Seduction.*

Sweeping the World

Perhaps "Babylon the great" spoken of in Revelation 18 refers to the re-emergence of a literal city of mystical practice and idolatry in the last days, but, at the very least, it must refer to a state of affairs that will sweep the world. Mysticism will be practiced on a global scale. And, all the while, the masses will be thinking they are pleasing God by practicing mysticism, oftentimes with the aid of drugs.

Then, this chapter in Revelation brings out one final point where it says:

> And in her was found the blood of prophets, and of saints, and of all that were slain upon the earth. (Revelation 18:24)

May I point out once again that mysticism (or occultism) connects one with a spirit world inhabited by demons posing to be angels of light. The occultist Alice Bailey, under the influence of her spirit guides, predicted that while New Age-style meditation will be promoted and propelled by the apostate Christian church, Christians who will not forsake the fundamentals of the faith will be seen as being in the way of bringing in this Age of enlightenment—an age of peace where everyone sees his or her own divinity and oneness with all things (which is, incidentally, the "fruit" of contemplative prayer). New Age leader Barbara Marx Hubbard suggests that these resisters of the new world/new reformation will be like a cancer that needs to be excised out of the Earth. She calls this elimination the "Selection Process."[6] Now I ask, what can be more hypocritical and diabolical than to think that the annihilation of godly people will bring about peace?

"The Regeneration of the Churches"

Yet, more and more Christians are joining in contemplative or mystical prayer, thinking it will make them stronger spiritually when the opposite is the case. In fact, what Christians are being drawn into is very antichrist in nature. Our research shows that those who engage in contemplative prayer, in time see less and less relevance to the Cross (the atonement) to where it becomes unnecessary. The reason for this is quite simple: contemplative prayer makes a person feel one with and a part of God to where a sacrifice for sin no longer makes any sense. As one New Age mystic said, "The era of the Single Savior is over."[7]

Shamanism, contemplative prayer, and New Age meditation are one and the same thing. As one adherent of mysticism explains, "The meditation of advanced occultists is identical with the prayer of advanced mystics."[8] Thomas Merton identified with Buddhism (saying he "intend[ed] to become as good a Buddhist as [he] can")[9] because he realized that the prayer of the Buddhist monks was the same as his. Alice Bailey, whom I consider the "mother" of the New Age movement, predicted that New Age (or occultic) spirituality would not enter the world by going *around* the Christian church but rather *through* it. She called it "the regeneration of the churches."[10] In explaining this, Ray Yungen says:

> Occultic prayer all over the world is coming to a head and bringing about the great falling away that the Bible predicts will happen.

> [I]nstead of opposing Christianity, the occult would capture and blend itself with Christianity and then use it as its primary vehicle for spreading and instilling New Age consciousness![11]

In other words, occultic prayer all over the world is coming to a head and bringing about the great falling away that the Bible predicts will happen. Modern-day proponents refer to it as *quantum spirituality*, and through borrowing terms used in physics, they tell us that if enough people meditate at the same time, we will achieve a *critical mass,* and we will then witness the dawning of the Age of Aquarius where peace will guide our planet. However, Alice Bailey and New Age leaders who adhere to the same beliefs see Christians who do not practice New Age-style meditation as in the way because they are not being "vibrationally sympathetic."[12] Such people, they maintain, will have to be eliminated!

In His Will or Abandoning Truth?

What will be the end of this resurrected city of Babylon? Revelation says:

> Therefore shall her plagues come in one day, death, and mourning, and famine; and she shall be utterly burned with fire: for strong is the Lord God who judgeth her. (Revelation 18:8)

And again it says, "for in one hour is thy judgment come" (Revelation 18:10). Apparently, the judgment to come will be speedy and severe.

So, while we can only speculate on the details of what will happen, we can be sure that a massive delusion will encompass the world and that severe judgment will also take place. Just knowing this, let us, as believers in the Lord Jesus Christ, cling all the more dearly to the Word of God and the Gospel message. Jesus died on the Cross to save sinners and rose from the dead to conquer death; our hope is in Him and nowhere or no one else. And while it is scary to think of persecution of the believers, it is more frightening to think of God's judgment on those who abandon God's Word for a lie. May we remember that no matter what we might suffer as Christians, the safest place to be is in God's will. Knowing this, let us encourage one another with the comfort and hope that is in the Lord.

Drugs, Meditation & "A Fully Developed Spirituality"

At Lighthouse Trails, we have a sense of urgency to call all Christians to return to their true roots. Our loyalty needs to be with our Savior and not with the traditions of men.

> Looking for that blessed hope, and the glorious appearing of the great God and our Saviour Jesus Christ; Who gave himself for us, that he might redeem us from all iniquity, and purify unto himself a peculiar people, zealous of good works. (Titus 2:13-14)

My hope is built on nothing less
Than Jesus' blood and righteousness;
I dare not trust the sweetest frame,
But wholly lean on Jesus' name.

Refrain:
On Christ, the solid Rock, I stand:
All other ground is sinking sand;
All other ground is sinking sand.

When darkness veils his lovely face,
I rest on his unchanging grace;
In every high and stormy gale,
My anchor holds within the veil. [Refrain]

His oath, his covenant, his blood,
Support me in the whelming flood;
When all around my soul gives way,
He then is all my hope and stay. [Refrain]

When he shall come with trumpet sound,
O may I then in him be found:
Dressed in his righteousness alone,
Faultless to stand before the throne. [Refrain]

Edward Mote (1834)

Chapter 7

Calvinism, Catholicism, Or Blessed Assurance— Which One Will It Be?

When I was a boy, about eight years old, a stranger in a Safeway grocery store parking lot gave my mother a plaque he had cast of plaster of paris that bore the words, "In all thy ways acknowledge him, and he shall direct thy paths" (Proverbs 3:6). As I mentioned in an earlier chapter, my mother had a special devotion to the Lord because as a child of about twelve years of age, after losing both her parents to mushroom poisoning, she knelt alone in a small chapel in Poland and invited Jesus into her heart. This was not something she was told to do but rather something she longed to do that she might have the life-long companionship of God in a world that had enclosed her with loneliness. There was something unique about her relationship with God in that it was somewhat spontaneous and very personal, though she had been raised in the Catholic Church where being Catholic meant going to Mass and receiving Christ in the sacrament of the Eucharist. Her strong belief in Jesus being the Son of God giving His life on the Cross for the sins of the world always burned in her heart as she knew Him as her personal Savior—sadly, something most Catholics miss due to the Catholic Church's misrepresentation of the Gospel.

And, like most Catholics, I too missed the meaning of the true Gospel (a gift entirely from God that offers redemption fully and salvation freely to all who put their trust in Christ).

My mother hung that plaque on our wall, and it became a witness to me that God was available and desired to have a personal relationship with me. At the age of 22, while serving in the U.S. Army in Germany, I too invited Jesus into my heart knowing He had died for all my sins and was inviting me into a new life with Him.[1]

Some years after my mother had received Christ in Poland as a young girl, she received word from her uncle in Portland, Oregon that he very much wanted her to live with him until she could establish herself on her own. He made all the arrangements for her to cross the Atlantic to New York harbor and from there to go by train to Portland, Oregon (where she would later meet my father). Shortly after her excursion from Poland, Hitler's troops invaded the country; chances are great that she may have never survived the war if she had stayed because the area in Poland where she grew up was closely bordering Germany. But God knew, and He provided the way of escape.

Ironically, fifty years after my mother received the Lord, I was in Germany and likewise invited Jesus into my heart and within that year, having completed my service in the military, returned home to Portland, Oregon.

While in Germany, I too encountered some life-threatening challenges, but God delivered me from these dangers. Looking back, I can see His handiwork in my life. I can only affirm that God is love and God is faithful. As Jeremiah declared during a most turbulent time in Jewish history:

> It is of the LORD's mercies that we are not consumed, because his compassions fail not. They [His mercies] are new every morning: great is thy faithfulness. (Lamentations 3:22-23)

The True Nature or a Distorted View of God

One thing I have learned in my walk with the Lord is that it is crucial that we attribute to God His very nature because we, as believers, take on the shape of our depiction of God. John Calvin depicted God as a monster, and he himself became a monster. Read the bio of his theology, life, and ministry, and you will see this is true.[2] It is both fortunate and conversely unfortunate that our view of God has a way of shaping us. There is a danger to the hardening of the heart that can occur if we entertain our minds with depictions of God that are not real. The resulting damage to the soul can be extreme as the Psalmist declares:

> With the merciful thou wilt shew thyself merciful; with an upright man thou wilt shew thyself upright; With the pure thou wilt shew thyself pure; and with the froward thou wilt shew thyself froward. For thou wilt save the afflicted people; but wilt bring down high looks. (Psalm 18:25-27)

God will bring down high looks, but He will bless those who bless Him, who esteem Him, and who attribute to Him His true nature. And to view God as an unloving hard-hearted deity or the author of sin (as John Calvin did) is nothing short of blasphemy.

A Powerful Yet Dangerous System

Calvinism is perhaps the most powerful force sweeping through the church today as it has been revived as never before—now promoted in most Bible colleges and seminaries. We often hear from proponents of Calvinism that the reason they embrace Calvinism is because it is the one thing that offers a full assurance of salvation, but the only true assurance of salvation is in knowing that God is faithful to His Word.

Even though the word "predestination" is not used in the Bible to directly signify salvation (I will explain this later), John Calvin used it to formulate a gospel of complete assurance. His idea was that God has already decided who will go to Heaven and who will go to Hell, and there is nothing anyone (including yourself) can do about it. This, in one sense, is very comforting if you can know that you are among the "elect." But the problem is that, while this may seem very comforting to the novice, Calvinist scholars understand, as did John Calvin himself, that this "belief" system actually offers no true assurance at all because it is impossible to know if you are among the elect. The only thing you can be sure of with this system is that if you are "predestined for Hell," you are sure to go there because that is God's "pleasure," and there is absolutely nothing you can do about it.

> At the present moment Calvinism may be the greatest danger because it looks very innocent.

It is interesting to note here that the Hegelian Formula (a branch of philosophy) states that when a thesis (an idea) is combined with an anti-thesis (a counter idea), the resulting synthesis achieves a higher level of truth; but with Christianity, when truth is mixed with error or light with darkness, the resulting grey area is very dangerous as Harry Ironside pointed out:

> Error is like leaven of which we read, "A little leaven leaveneth the whole lump" (Galatians 5:9). Truth mixed with error is equivalent to all error, except that it is more innocent looking and, therefore, more dangerous. God hates such a mixture! Any error, or any truth-and-error mixture, calls for definite exposure and repudiation. To condone such is to be unfaithful to God and His Word and treacherous to imperiled souls for whom Christ died.[3]

Calvinism, Catholicism, or Blessed Assurance

I fear for the church of today; and I think that perhaps at the present moment Calvinism may be the greatest danger because, just as Ironside describes, it looks very innocent. In fact, over the years Calvinism has been building momentum as its leaders have grasped the Olympic torch of academia and "biblical" scholarship and run with it. Consequently, many who are looking for a deeper and biblical walk with the Lord are embracing it, which Bible colleges and seminaries are welcoming with open arms. Indeed, many of today's biblical scholars are Calvinists who like to quote John Calvin's axiom *sola scriptura* to maintain that truth is found only in the Scriptures.

However, the sad truth about John Calvin is that while he was correct in asserting that spiritual truths need to be derived solely from Scripture, his life and ministry (theology) largely contradicted the Bible. In life, he started his own inquisition in Geneva where he was directly or indirectly involved with the tortuous deaths of dozens of people, whose crimes were to disagree with his convoluted teachings. Among those whom he most hated were the Anabaptists who disagreed with his practice of infant baptism. His theology was excised largely, not from Scripture but from the writings of Augustine (a Greek philosopher turned Christian). While Augustine did much to reshape biblical Christianity into what became the doctrines of the Roman Catholic Church and the foundations of Medieval thought, John Calvin hopped the train of the Reformation and embedded in it the doctrines of his tainted thinking.

Earthly Wisdom and Foolish Philosophy

Before I go any further, please allow me to offer my observations on philosophy, having been a student of philosophy myself. Oftentimes, philosophers will frown at Christianity as lacking logic. In the case of Augustine having formerly been a Greek philosopher, he thought he could use his skills of logic to reformulate Christianity into its various doctrines expressed in a logical and orderly manner. But the problem is not that Christianity is illogical but that we typically lack the insight to tackle spiritual matters using earthly logic. Even Paul, whom I consider to be the greatest theologian of all time, spoke of his own understanding when he said, "For now we see through a glass, darkly; but then face to face: now I know in part; but then shall I know even as also I am known" (1 Corinthians 13:12).

Paul found great wisdom and insight in Christianity though he had formerly persecuted the church. When he encountered the Greek philosophers on Mars Hill,[4] they were much entertained by his thinking, but they could never wrap their minds around the simplicity of the Gospel. That is why Paul could say:

> For the preaching of the cross is to them that perish foolishness; but unto us which are saved it is the power of God. For it is written, I will destroy the wisdom of the wise, and will bring to nothing the understanding of the prudent. Where is the wise? where is the scribe? where is the disputer of this world? hath not God made foolish the wisdom of this world?
>
> For after that in the wisdom of God the world by wisdom knew not God, it pleased God by the foolishness of preaching to save them that believe. For the Jews require a sign, and the Greeks seek after wisdom: But we preach Christ crucified, unto the Jews a stumbling block, and unto the Greeks foolishness; But unto them which are called, both Jews and Greeks, Christ the power of God, and the wisdom of God. Because the foolishness of God is wiser than men; and the weakness of God is stronger than men.
>
> For ye see your calling, brethren, how that not many wise men after the flesh, not many mighty, not many noble, are called: But God hath chosen the foolish things of the world to confound the wise; and God hath chosen the weak things of the world to confound the things which are

mighty; And base things of the world, and things which are despised, hath God chosen, yea, and things which are not, to bring to nought things that are: That no flesh should glory in his presence. But of him are ye in Christ Jesus, who of God is made unto us wisdom, and righteousness, and sanctification, and redemption. (1 Corinthians 1:18-30)

For I am not ashamed of the gospel of Christ: for it is the power of God unto salvation to every one that believeth; to the Jew first, and also to the Greek. (Romans 1:16)

The real problem the philosophers of Paul's time had was not that they were too smart for Paul but that the one and true God who created everything was, in their case "THE UNKNOWN GOD. Whom . . . ye ignorantly worship" (Acts 17:23); and most of them were too proud to really hear Paul. Pride has a way of stopping the ears of the proud while the humble have ears to hear: "Howbeit certain men clave unto him, and believed" (Acts 17:34). The folly of the proud was that they trusted in their *own* wisdom, making their skills at reason and dialogue their own god and final authority.

As far as we can know, Calvin most likely never came to a saving knowledge of the Lord Jesus Christ. He, too, fell under the spell of exalting his own reasoning above the truth of the Gospel while looking to the writings of Augustine to confirm his errant thought to be true. Although he considered himself to be a humble man, his ruthless and demonic way of treating Christians who disagreed with his thinking reflects a whole other side to John Calvin that Calvinists would want to dismiss, but this is also at the peril of countless people who look to Calvinism to secure their own salvation. Consider, for example, some words Calvin addressed to God in his will shortly before he died in 1564:

> I testify also and profess that I humbly seek from God, <u>*that He may so will me*</u> to be washed and purified by the

great Redeemer's blood, *shed for the sins of the human race,* that it may be permitted me to stand before His tribunal under the covert of the Redeemer Himself.⁵ (italics in original; underline added)

Though he here refers to himself as "humbly" seeking God for his own salvation, the words "that He may so will me" betray the contradictory and fatalistic nature of Calvin's belief and conduct. While he acknowledges the efficacy of Jesus' death on the Cross for the sins of mankind, he refuses to recognize its availability to all as revealed in all Scripture, particularly the Gospels.

Consider, for example, how Jesus, in speaking to the Samaritan woman at the well, referred to the salvation He was offering as water freely given—as "a well of water springing up into everlasting life" (John 4:14). The Jewish religious leaders of the day frowned upon the Samaritans, and the path to Heaven they offered was paved with many obstacles and burdens too heavy to carry. Sadly, and as Paul warned would happen, the apostate "Christian" church soon followed after them, placing heavy yokes upon believers and distorting the truth of the Gospel. It wasn't that long before the Roman Catholic Church began to form, claiming that Peter had been their first pope and absorbing much of the teachings and doctrines, not from the Bible, but from so-called "church fathers" and mystics who received much of their inspiration from mind-altering techniques borrowed from the east.⁶

This abandonment of the Scriptures led, as we should expect, not to revival but to a period in Western history known by terms such as "the middle ages," "the medieval period," or "the dark ages." This was also a period of history when the Scriptures were withheld from the people and only spoon-fed by the clergy, who were deemed the only ones able to properly interpret the Bible. This period was marked by crusades conducted with sword and spear and inquisitions conducted under papal authority by fire and unbelievable tortures. The demons laughed as they witnessed the fruit of their labors. Long forgotten were Scriptures like 1 John 4:8 that says, "He that loveth not knoweth not God; for God is love."

Ironically, Calvin, who claimed to be a reformer, followed suit and became what was known as "the Protestant Pope" with a reputation spanning continental Europe, though his treatment of humanity was brutal.

Words nearly fail me to express my heart-felt sense of dismay and urgency at the tremendous loss to the true Gospel reaching the hearts of God's people.

The Calvinist "Gospel"

As a Christian, there are two things that concern me most greatly. The first, as it should be, is for the Gospel to reach the unsaved as it really is, unpolluted by human "wisdom" and innovations. The second is for Christians to recognize how much of what we call "the church" has diverged from the truth and simplicity of the Gospel.

I don't question that there are a good number of Catholics (like my mother) and Calvinists (who are growing exponentially in number) who are truly saved, but they are saved only because they have put their trust in Jesus who shed His blood at Calvary to redeem us and cleanse us from all sin. But I fear for those who have never actually put their faith in Christ for His free gift of salvation—simple and uncomplicated—but have exchanged it for burdensome religion founded on earthly logic and philosophical reasoning. As a former Catholic, I know all too well that the Catholic version of the Gospel is not founded on the one-time sacrifice of Christ at Calvary (as described in chapters 9 and 10 in Hebrews) and received by faith alone but on the works-based sacraments, in particular the sacrament of the Eucharist where Christ is re-sacrificed daily at the altar as a "non-bloody sacrifice." This sacrament offers a way to earn the free gift of salvation. All this is contradictory to the Scriptures and to true logic.

Likewise, Calvinism requires that the Scriptures be altered to create its own version of the Gospel. In a nutshell, Calvinism is actually the philosophic religion of fatalism. Its chief precept is that God has unalterably predetermined who will go to Heaven or Hell. Its formulation is philosophic logic that goes like this:

Premise: God is sovereign, and everything He does is for His pleasure. If God is sovereign, then everything that happens in the universe and all creation is His will. If everything is His will, then:

- God is the author of all good.

- God is the author of all evil.

- God is the author of sin.

- God delights in sending people to Heaven.

- God also delights in sending many more to Hell.

Hence, if all the above is true, then man can have no free will. The reasoning, as one can see, is a continuous chain of thought that goes on and on, which could lead us to one final conclusion: If God can only be sovereign *when* everything is His will, then He has given everyone absolutely *no* free will. He makes people sin and then punishes them in an eternal Hell for sinning—and this is all for God's pleasure. Sadly, this is what the *more seasoned* Calvinists are teaching. In doing so, they are describing God as a monster, yet I don't know of any Calvinist who would admit to this. But this is what they do, continually and all the time. God is insulted, even blasphemed, yet they do not seem to know they are doing it. That is delusion. It is what happens to Calvinists who have allowed human logic to overrule a heart-felt appreciation they should have for who God really is—a God of love.

Though it is claimed to be so, there is no actual eternal security in Calvinism. Just as with philosophical fatalism, Calvinistic fatalism works in the same way in that we are all doomed/chosen to what God has already ordained for us, and there is nothing we can do to change that.

The problem with Calvin's "God" is that "He" is totally unbiblical and incomparable to the God of the Bible. According to the Bible, "God is light, and in him is no darkness at all" (1 John 1:5); He has never and will never sin; therefore, He cannot be the author of sin or evil. "God is love" (1 John 4:8); therefore, there is no wickedness with God. Calvin was a wicked man, having lived the life of a despot, but his wickedness was his own doing and only reflected the character of the god of his own imagination. When Calvinist teacher, A.W. Pink says that no one can resist the will of God,[7] this would even mean that someone like Hitler was not able to resist God's will and that he (Hitler) was only doing what God wanted him to do. How could God be called just and righteous for not only causing men to do evil but then condemning them for doing what they could not even control?

Calvin's God Too Small

There is another difference between Calvin's god and the God of the Bible: Calvin's god is too small. His god could only be sovereign if man had no free will. The only way Calvin's god could be sovereign would be if man were a puppet on a string with God pulling the strings. The God of the Bible is much greater and more powerful than this. He can be sovereign, even though He has given man free will, while God's light penetrates the darkness of our world; and He is brilliant enough to work all things together for good. While the God of the Bible is big enough to be sovereign even while man has free will, Calvin's god lacks the ability, greatness, and intelligence to do this. The more one studies Calvinism, the more apparent it becomes that to make the Calvinist scenario work, extensive alteration of not only the Scriptures but of God Himself must take place.

The Foundation

The foundation of one's faith is always what's most important, just as the foundation of a building is most critical. What is the foundation of the Christian faith? It is Jesus Himself as presented in the Gospel. The Gospel tells us that when we place our faith and trust in Christ, who paid the penalty for the sins of the whole world, God forgives us, cleanses us, and we are born again as the Holy Spirit now indwells us. This salvation is freely given because Jesus paid the price of our redemption in full, way back at Calvary. The words "New Testament" is a legal term that really means "New Covenant" whereby God inscribes His righteous nature on the tablet of our hearts in place of the tablets of stone Moses gave—which exposed the sinfulness of man's heart but lacked the power to transform us to a godly nature.

Having been raised as a Catholic, I can see now that the foundation of my faith as a Catholic was not in trusting in the one-time sacrifice of Christ at Calvary but in the continual re-sacrificing of Christ in the sacrament of the Eucharist (communion) and my participation in it. There was never an altar call for me to come to receive Christ by faith and be born again because I was taught that I was already a Christian by virtue of having been baptized as a baby. Not until I was 22 did I recognize that I was lost and needed to receive Christ as my Savior. I should add, however, that while the Roman Catholic Church still adheres to salvation through participation in the sacraments with the Eucharist being the focal point of the Mass, Catholicism is gradually being transformed through mysticism and aligning itself with New Age practices and beliefs. Roman Catholicism has never claimed that one can be assured of one's salvation. Being works based, it sees such assurance as being presumptuous and prideful. The inroads of mysticism into the church perhaps is filling that void of assurance in that New Age mysticism is pantheistic (or panentheistic) in believing that we are one with and a part of God and therefore in no need of a savior.

Calvinism, Catholicism, or Blessed Assurance

In the case of Calvinism, John Calvin's foundation for the faith was his doctrine of predestination which, like the sacrament of the Eucharist, looks innocent but ends up placing a barrier between us and our ability to receive the Gospel. While the doctrine of predestination purports to offer assurance of salvation, in reality, it places doubts in the minds and hearts of people. The problem is that it is an unworthy substitute for the truth of the Gospel.

It should be noted that the word for predestination only appears four times in the Bible—in Romans 8:29 and 30 as predestinate and in Ephesians 1:5 and 11 as predestinated; and in none of these instances is it referring to the experience of salvation. In fact, Romans 8:30 draws a distinction between predestination and salvation by using separate terms: "Moreover whom he did predestinate . . . them he *also justified* (emphasis added). The meaning of the word "predestination" is actually found in the word itself: God has prepared a destination for the believer—for us to be like Christ "to be conformed to the image of his Son . . ." (Romans 8:29) and to "obtain an inheritance" (Ephesians 1:11). Paul goes on to say in Ephesians, "*after* that ye believed, *ye were sealed* with that holy Spirit of promise, which is the earnest of our inheritance until the redemption of the purchased possession . . ." (Ephesians 1:13-14; emphasis added). Here Paul is using legal language to say that God has prepared a place for those who put their trust in Christ! And Jesus did say, "I go to prepare a place for you" (John 14:2).

There is much comfort that can be derived from a proper understanding of predestination, while Calvin's understanding of the term plays havoc on the minds of seasoned Calvinists. Consider, for example, this confession from the late R.C. Sproul (d. 2017):

> A while back I had one of those moments . . . suddenly the question hit me: 'R.C., what if you are not one of the redeemed? What if your destiny is not heaven after all, but hell?' Let me tell you, that I was flooded in my body with

a chill that went from my head to the bottom of my spine. I was terrified.[8]

Sadly, R.C. Sproul was only being honest in that, having been one of the foremost Calvinist scholars of our time, he had a proper understanding of what Calvinism actually teaches. To the novice, Calvinism appears to be offering eternal security, but to the seasoned theologian, there is every reason to fear when Calvin's god delights in sending most people to Hell; and "believing" the Gospel is seen as ineffectual to this vast number of people already deemed to Hell.

Is There Assurance of Our Salvation?

It is frightening to see how so many people who profess to be Christians are falling into the delusions that are encompassing our world today. A while back, I was questioning, what is to keep *me* from becoming part of a world-wide delusion? After all, Jesus Himself warned that in the last days massive delusion will sweep the Earth.

The fact is, we do need to guard our hearts, and no one is assured of getting everything right. But at the same time, we have a haven of safety in the Lord. I think the secret is to come to God as a child—that is in child-like faith and simple humility. Though the Bible warns of a massive world-wide delusion in the last days, the Bible also is filled with warnings and exhortations, both in the Old and New Testaments, to steer clear of the massive deceptions of the day. All these promptings from Scripture indicate that God does *not will* this deception in our lives and offers His protection to all who take refuge

> The Bible is filled with warnings and exhortations to steer clear of the massive deceptions of the day.

in Him. The Bible says, "But he giveth more grace, Wherefore he saith, God resisteth the proud, but giveth grace unto the humble" (James 4:6).

We can, therefore, flee the deceit of the world if we flee to God. It is important to know there is one thing God magnifies above His own name as the psalmist describes, "I will worship toward thy holy temple, and praise thy name for thy lovingkindness and for thy truth: for thou hast magnified thy word above all thy name" (Psalm 138:2). Why would God do this? Well, for God to be high above all that exists and to be fully worthy of all esteem, He must be completely faithful to all His Word and all His promises. Properly understood, this means that if you read John 3:16 and believe it, you have complete assurance in your salvation because God is completely faithful to His Word.

The Spirit of Antichrist

The history of Christianity has been marred by errant teachings. Paul predicted this would happen when he said:

> For I know this, that after my departing shall grievous wolves enter in among you, not sparing the flock. Also of your own selves shall men arise, speaking perverse things, to draw away disciples after them. (Acts 20:29-30)

The apostle John adds further illumination on the subject describing how the spirit of antichrist present in his day would be infused in human history before the coming of the Antichrist:

> Little children, it is the last time: and as ye have heard that antichrist shall come, even now are there many antichrists; whereby we know that it is the last time. (1 John 2:18)

> Every spirit that confesseth not that Jesus Christ is come in the flesh is not of God: and this is that spirit of antichrist,

whereof ye have heard that it should come; and even now already is it in the world. (1 John 4:3)

It is valuable to know and to recognize that the spirit of antichrist has been working over the centuries. Too often, we don't see the spirit of antichrist working because we expect to see something sensational, but the antichrist spirit is not always expressed as vehement rage and anger over Jesus Christ. The Greek prefix *ante* can indicate hatred and opposition, but it can also signify a substitute; and this is where the enemy can sneak in through the back door. Antichrist can be a person or a teaching that is in place of or a substitute for Christ—a false imitation Christ. Ultimately, Satan's scheme is to take as many people to Hell as he can, so his target has always been to corrupt the Gospel and discredit Jesus Christ for who He is and His redeeming sacrifice at Calvary. This is why we have witnessed so much distortion of the simple Gospel that Jesus really does save, and He does it very well, especially in that Jesus sealed the new covenant with His own blood two thousand years ago as an irrevocable covenant. The Old Covenant required daily and yearly sacrifices pointing to the one-time perfect and complete sacrifice to come later. All this proves that our salvation is very secure when we place our hope and trust in Christ.

Blessed Assurance

My mother, who passed away on July 4th, 1996, was a great witness and strength to me in the years I knew her after my return from the Army as a born-again Christian. As a young believer, it took me several years to sort out the problems with Catholicism, and I was thus not able to share much with her on its doctrinal problems before she began to develop Alzheimer's disease. But we would talk, and she agreed that salvation is something we can only secure in an abiding relationship with Christ; she believed Jesus' words that one must be born again to enter the Kingdom of God,

Calvinism, Catholicism, or Blessed Assurance

and even as her Alzheimer's progressed, she remembered doing that when she invited Jesus into her heart in Poland at a young age.

During the last years of her life, she was the most powerful witness to me of God's saving grace. Her mind was affected, but her spirit remained strong. She reached a point where she could not tell me my name nor even that I was her son. But she knew I was special to her, and she never wavered in her faith.

As the youngest in the family, I took on the role of taking Mom to church. However, as I came to a greater understanding of the serious errors of Roman Catholicism, I felt increasingly more uncomfortable about taking her to a Roman Catholic church, which I had come to realize was an apostate church. Having friends and family members who were Catholic, I knew if I took her to a "non-Catholic church," they would see it as manipulating her in her weakened mental faculties. But having found a good Gospel-preaching church, I carefully explained to my mother my plan, and twice she told me she would rather go to the new church than the Catholic church. I must confess I was a bit nervous on that day when she sat, for the first time, in a Gospel-centered church. As the worship songs began, I wondered if she would be OK with it or want to leave. Then as the singing progressed, and some people were raising their hands in worship, I took a peek from the corner of my eye to see how she was doing; I then saw that her eyes were bright as she bore a smile on her face—and her hands were lifted up too!

In her final days, I truly witnessed the grace of God in her life. Having lost so much of her cognitive skills, she was totally dependent on the Lord for His saving power. Spiritually speaking, there was practically nothing she could do other than be dependent on the Lord. Yet, at the same time, she was happy and unafraid as if the Lord had taken full responsibility for the safety of her soul—and, indeed, that is exactly what He did.

Seeing what the Lord was doing in her life created for me a sharp contrast to a lot of what I was witnessing happening in the church.

Christian authors were pumping out new books providing *newly discovered* anecdotes on how to live a successful Christian life—everywhere there was a new formula for success. My mother, who could participate in none of these "secrets," was secure in the love of God. I'm not saying that everything written during this time was theologically wrong, but what I am saying is that, over the years, much of the church has lost its first love, and instead of being grounded in the simplicity of the Gospel and our Savior's love, it has been looking to the latest formula or gimmick.

In all his writings from the Gospel of John to his epistles to the Book of Revelation, the apostle John expresses the assurance we have in Christ. He, like Paul and the other apostles, saw the power of the Gospel to eternally save those who put their faith in Christ. If this were not so, then John could not have penned words with such resolve as this:

> If we receive the witness of men, the witness of God is greater: for this is the witness of God which he hath testified of his Son. He that believeth on the Son of God hath the witness in himself: he that believeth not God hath made him a liar; because he believeth not the record that God gave of his Son. And this is the record, that God hath given to us eternal life, and this life is in his Son. He that hath the Son hath life; and he that hath not the Son of God hath not life. These things have I written *unto you that believe* on the name of the Son of God; *that ye may know* that ye have eternal life, and *that ye may believe* on the name of the Son of God. (1 John 5:9-13; emphasis added)

God's testimony is much stronger than that of mere men. What's more, God has taken His own testimony and made it into a testament, a legally binding contract, sealed in His own blood, and upheld by His holy Word that He magnifies above His own name. Unfortunately, over the last two thousand years, there have been too many wolves in sheep's clothing who have tried to defuse the power of the Gospel by saying it is insufficient or needs help (as with Catholicism in its daily "unbloody sacrifice" of the Eucharist) or superseded (as with Calvinism in its own philosophical version of fatalism). But for those who reach out to God, He is always there, for Christ has forever settled the destiny of those who place their trust in Him.

God's grace is readily available to the humble heart as I saw in my mother's life. I witnessed not only God's saving power in her life but also His *keeping* power. May we realize that power and that blessed assurance today, for it *is* the power of the Gospel.

> That it might be fulfilled which was spoken by the prophet, saying, I will open my mouth in parables; I will utter things which have been kept secret from the foundation of the world. (Matthew 13:35)
>
> I will open my mouth in a parable: I will utter dark sayings of old. (Psalm 78:2)

Chapter 8

A Potter Looks at Romans 9

Have you ever wondered why Jesus spoke in parables? Concerning the Messiah to come, the Old Testament indicated He would open His mouth in parables. And throughout His ministry, Jesus used countless illustrations in His teachings. For some, He became a "stumbling block and a rock of offence" even as He shared spiritual truths with earthly illustrations. And I've pondered from time to time of both the positive impact to those who understood and the negative repercussions of those who took His statements the wrong way. As an ex-Roman Catholic, I am particularly concerned with how one takes His statement, "I am the bread of life" (John 6:35) because I understand now that His statement was spiritual and not physical (see John 6:63). But, over the centuries, the Roman Catholic Church has persecuted, tortured, and even executed many people over this very point.

Before making the above statement, Jesus had the following discourse with the people who were flocking to Him:

> Verily, verily, I say unto you, Ye seek me, not because ye saw the miracles, but because ye did eat of the loaves,

and were filled. Labour not for the meat which perisheth, but for that meat which endureth unto everlasting life, which the Son of man shall give unto you: for him hath God the Father sealed. Then said they unto him, What shall we do, that we might work the works of God? Jesus answered and said unto them, This is the work of God, *that ye believe on him whom he hath sent.* (John 6:26-29; emphasis added)

From the above dialogue, it becomes clear that Jesus wanted them to believe the Gospel. The Gospel was never intended to become a works-based religion of literally ingesting Jesus in the sacrament of the Eucharist but the Good News that God bestows eternal life to those who put their trust in the complete and finished work of Christ at Calvary in redeeming us from our sins. Unfortunately, even though Scripture refutes an earthy, physical view of how God redeems us, people remain blind to the meaning of the Gospel until they humbly and whole-heartedly turn to Christ. Until then, there is no assurance of salvation because they have never laid hold of it.

Likewise, Calvinism offers a distorted view of salvation based largely on a misconceived idea of what God is like. And while Catholicism is rooted in a misconstrued perception of what John 6 is talking about, Calvinism, similarly, is founded on a misconstrued view of what Romans 9 is talking about. In fact, Calvinist leaders will often guide their students to Romans 9 (isolating it from other Scriptures) because it is one of the very few passages in Scripture that remotely appears to support the conclusions of John Calvin— namely that man really has no free will, and consequently anything and everything that happens on planet Earth has been preordained by God and is according to His own good pleasure; in essence, according to this view, it is God's good pleasure to send most people to Hell. Romans 9 is often used to lure unsuspecting people into debates about predestination in that it gives the Calvinist a sense of security that he will win his hearer to his side.

This, of course, is a misuse of Scripture because while Romans 9, when isolated from the rest of Scripture, may seem to hold to the fatalistic viewpoint of Calvinism, the whole of Scripture absolutely refutes the findings and conclusions of John Calvin. Like Calvin, the Calvinist is now left with a lifelong task of having to read all of Scripture through a filter, where the meanings of words must be altered and Scriptures twisted and distorted to fit the Calvinist view.

It is therefore often unproductive to try to have any intelligent debate by looking only at Romans 9 as it seems to defy resolution by mulling over it in isolation from the rest of Scripture.

A Refutation

However, there is a passage in Jeremiah that not only refutes Calvinism, it also addresses Romans 9. And while there are countless Scriptures that equally refute Calvinism, this passage has special significance because it speaks of the potter referred to in Romans 9:19-23 where Paul uses the illustration of a potter in similar fashion to why Jesus spoke in parables. The things of God, being spiritual, are often difficult to understand and can often be best explained by way of illustration. However, earthly illustrations need to be nonetheless spiritually discerned as we have already seen in Jesus' referral to Himself as "the bread of life." We must, therefore, take care not to distort an illustration from its actual and intended meaning.

With that said, let's take a look at Jeremiah 18:1-12:

> The *word which came* to Jeremiah *from the* LORD, saying, Arise, and go down to the potter's house, and there I will cause thee to hear my words. Then I went down to the potter's house, and, behold, he wrought a work on the wheels. *And the vessel that he made of clay was marred in*

the hand of the potter: so he *made it again* another vessel, *as seemed good to the potter* to make it.

Then the word of the LORD came to me, saying, O house of Israel, *cannot I do with you as this potter?* saith *the* LORD. Behold, as the clay is in the potter's hand, so are ye in mine hand, O house of Israel. At what instant I shall speak concerning a nation, and concerning a kingdom, to pluck up, and to pull down, and to destroy it; *If that nation,* against whom I have pronounced, *turn from their evil, I will repent of the evil that I thought to do unto them.*

And at what instant I shall speak concerning a nation, and concerning a kingdom, to build and to plant it; *If it do evil* in my sight, that it obey not my voice, *then I will repent of the good, wherewith I said I would benefit them.* Now therefore go to, speak to the men of Judah, and to the inhabitants of Jerusalem, saying, Thus saith the LORD; Behold, I frame evil against you, and devise a device against you: *return ye now every one from his evil way, and make your ways and your doings good.* And they said, *There is no hope: but we will walk after our own devices, and we will every one do the imagination of his evil heart.* (emphasis added)

First of all, we should establish who the potter is in this passage. Rather than giving Jeremiah a vision, God instructed him to observe an actual potter at work. However, we learn in verse 6 that this potter served as an illustration of God as the potter of humanity—something that is both symbolic and quite literal. For in Genesis 2:7, we read that "the LORD God formed man of the dust of the ground" making Him a potter in a literal sense of unequaled skill and intelligence. The capitalized word "LORD" refers to Jehovah of the Old Testament whom John refers to as "the Word" in the New Testament who created all things (John 1:3) and "was made flesh, and dwelt among us" (v. 14), referring to Jesus. The same word for "Lord" is also what is used in this passage from Jeremiah, which identifies this Potter as our Creator who later became man to be our Redeemer.

Now, even though our bodies are mere clay, God did a wondrous work in creating us with an eternal soul (Genesis 2:7) fashioned after His own image (Genesis 1:26). And, while Genesis 1 and 2 are somewhat ambiguous as to what it means to be created in God's image, Jeremiah 18 gives us insight into how we were created.

It should be pointed out here that while the potter Jeremiah was observing was doing something physical, the work of the Potter referred to as "Lord" is doing a work that is spiritual. The spiritual "clay" really has to do with the fact that God has created all of us with a free will. The idea of free will actually makes a lot of sense from the perspective of God as our Potter (Creator) because if God had created us without it, we would be no more than puppets pleasing God, not because we want to but because we would, in effect, be forced to do His will. But Scripture says that "God loveth a cheerful giver" as opposed to one who gives "grudgingly, or of *necessity*" (see 2 Corinthians 9:7; emphasis added). This, of course, makes complete sense even from a human perspective in that love—given or received— takes on full meaning when it is done freely and by choice.

So God made us of a spiritual "clay" that includes free will. However, this presents a dichotomy for the spiritual Potter in that He now has a substance ("clay") to work with that is mutually exclusive of the results. For just as the earthly potter finds inconsistency in the clay he uses, the spiritual Potter must deal with the inconsistency of free will in the spiritual clay He uses to create and sustain life in each individual. Such is the situation in Jeremiah 18 where the potter Jeremiah is observing may have exceedingly great skill yet finds that "the vessel that he made of clay was marred in the hand of the potter" (v. 4); but rather than throw the clay away, he reworks the same clay again into "another vessel, as seemed good to the potter to make it" (v. 4). That is to say, he reshaped the clay into a vessel that still seemed good to him though it had failed to take the shape of what he originally designed.

Such is the predicament of our spiritual Potter who fashioned each of us with a free will. But rather than throw us away, He works on us when we stray, refashioning our lives with the hope of repentance. We see this brought out dramatically in this passage from Jeremiah where God, speaking to the nation of Israel, gives opportunity after opportunity for repentance—both individually and as a people. Here God emphasizes that how we live our lives is not determined by our genes but on the choices we make. Ezekiel 18:1-4 elaborates on this point in referring to a proverb that suggested the iniquity of parents is locked into succeeding generations. In response to this, God says, "Behold, all souls are mine; as the soul of the father, so also the soul of the son is mine: the soul that sinneth, it shall die" (v. 4). In other words, everyone is responsible for him or herself, and it is our *own* iniquity that brings us down. Likewise, the opportunity for repentance is available to us all, just as God's forgiveness is available to all.

Designed by the Potter

Thus, as we ponder the workings of the spiritual Potter in Jeremiah 18, it becomes abundantly clear that He has no resemblance to the imaginings of John Calvin. While Calvin's "God" bestows no free will on all people, Jeremiah's God is opposite in designing us as our Potter. In fact, beginning with verse 5, it becomes clear it is God Himself speaking through Jeremiah, who will now describe Himself as our Potter. Speaking of entire nations, God says that if a wicked nation repents, He will "repent" of the judgment that He meant to bring upon it (vv. 7-8); likewise, if a godly nation turns to wickedness, God will "repent of the good, wherewith [He] said [He] would benefit them" (v. 10). Furthermore, in verse 11, God speaks to the individual when He says, "return ye now *every one* from his evil way, and make your ways and your *doings* good" (emphasis added). Here, it is abundantly clear that God sees man as having:

- A free will (otherwise He would not plead with them to repent).

- The ability to repent (again, why else would He ask them to repent?).

- The ability to do good (as seen in verse 11).

But the clay of Calvin is a crippled clay in that Calvin's creation has no free will (but must act out what God has predetermined him to do), is totally lacking in the ability to repent and believe, and is unable to do good (due to "total depravity"—the "T" in TULIP). Scripture says, "Repent ye therefore, and be converted, that your sins may be blotted out" (Acts 3:19) and "Believe on the Lord Jesus Christ, and thou shalt be saved" (Acts 16:31); but Calvinism says the opposite in that we must be converted first before we can repent and believe. Again, Scripture says, "godly sorrow worketh repentance to salvation" (2 Corinthians 7:10) and "the law was our schoolmaster to bring us unto Christ, that we might be justified by faith" (Galatians 3:24). What all this is saying is that we must come to Christ in order to be converted. Conviction of sin enables us to see our need of a Savior while

> Calvin's creation has no free will, is totally lacking in the ability to repent and believe, and is unable to do good.

putting our faith in Christ opens the door to receive Him (be converted, born again).

But Calvin has rendered us as a disabled clay totally unlike the clay of Jeremiah 18. It is no wonder we are now receiving testimonies here at Lighthouse Trails of people coming out of Calvinism who thought they could find strength and assurance in it but instead were left with fear and uncertainty.

Furthermore, Calvinism renders people ineffective for leading people to Christ.* As an example of this, I remember our neighbors we once had who belonged to the Reformed church who criticized us for reaching out to another neighbor with the Gospel because they had already decided the other neighbor was predetermined to go to Hell. Their son told us he was a Christian because he had been baptized into the Reformed church as a baby (as prescribed by Calvin), but he later turned to the occult, walking away from what he knew to be the Christian faith altogether. Calvinism also renders its members ineffective in that it actually presents another gospel than that taught in the Scriptures. Though Calvinist scholars have much to say, when all is said and done, their only conclusion is that there is only one assurance of salvation, and that is in knowing that they are of the elect; but they can *never* know if they are of the elect and are therefore left with doubt and fear. Assurance in the Cross has been superseded by election, which turns out to be no assurance at all.

---

*While there are Calvinists who are involved with evangelizing and mission work, it is not what most would think of evangelizing; the Calvinist who "witnesses" to others is merely hoping that he or she somehow is "witnessing" to one of the elect, who upon hearing about Christ will be "converted" and then able to believe on Christ. Many Calvinists do not like altar calls or open invitations to receive Christ because they fear it will draw too many "false converts" (i.e., the non-elect who make a profession of faith but who really aren't of the elect).

A Stumbling Block for the Calvinist

The problem for the Calvinist is that Romans 9, under the tutelage of John Calvin, has become a stumbling block for the Christian in much the same way that the Catholic Church has used John 6 to mean that we are saved through participation in Holy Communion. However, just as careful examination of John 6 in the context of the whole chapter and with the whole of Scripture will bring one to the Gospel, Romans 9 will bring one to the Gospel when properly understood.

Unfortunately, the Calvinist is left thinking that his doctrine is sound when he states, "We are saved 'by grace alone through faith alone'," when all the while under the Calvinist system, he is actually being "saved" by election alone under a very confused theology that turns the steps to salvation around backwards and makes the Cross inaccessible because free will has been made void. In fact, the only assurance he can have is in "the perseverance of the saints" (the "P" in TULIP), but that is no real assurance at all because he can never know if he persevered enough nor if he will persevere to the very end. Ironically, this system of believing is actually works-based and not by grace alone nor is it by faith alone. The Calvinist is caught in a system designed by John Calvin that appears as if it should work but in actuality places the "believer" in a life-long position of questions and doubt. And while there are Calvinists who will proudly go about saying, "I am of the elect," the truly honest and learned Calvinist knows in his heart that Calvinism offers no such assurance. That is why Calvin himself appealed to God before he died to show him mercy and grant him salvation—if God willed it.

So, even though I cannot relate to you the pain and damage of being raised Calvinist, I can as an ex-Roman Catholic comprehend what it means to take something beautiful in Scripture (i.e., the Gospel) and twist it to mean something else. It is the burden of exchanging the easy yoke of the Gospel for the heavy yoke of man.

If Romans 9 were not offering a Gospel to "whosoever will, let him take of the water of life freely" (Revelation 22:17) but rather only to a pre-selected few, at the very least, the immediate context of Romans 9 would support this. But, in fact, we find this is not so. On the contrary, Romans 9:7-8 indicates that the true children of Abraham are the children of promise (i.e., those who believe in the promises of God just as Abraham did). And while Romans 9:20-23 may seem perplexing, it can only make sense with the rest of Scripture that God was willing to endure (not delight in) the vessels fitted for destruction because He has created everyone with a free will. This is what is so aptly brought out in our Jeremiah 18 passage about the Potter. And, yes, God does have foreknowledge of those who will reject Him, but the decision to receive or reject God's promises nonetheless resides in the heart of man according to his own will. Hence, according to Romans 9:19-20, those who resist God *are guilty* because they have freely willed it to be so. As for salvation being freely given, Romans 9:30 goes so far as to say that salvation is available even to the Gentiles if they will but receive "the righteousness which is of faith." Then, in closing this chapter, Romans 9:31-33 speaks of the "stumblingstone and rock of offence" (v. 33) referred to earlier in our discussion. It is of paramount importance, therefore, that we do not play games with the Gospel. The Gospel is true, it is of promise, and it is available to whosoever wills it. Finally, Romans 9 ends with these words, "*[W]hosoever* believeth on him *shall not be ashamed* [disappointed]" (v. 33, emphasis added).

Moving beyond Romans 9, we do not have to look very far to find some of the most comforting and reassuring Scripture to support the idea that God's salvation is freely given to all who will come to Him. Romans 10:4 tells us that "Christ is the end of the law for righteousness to *every one* that believeth" (emphasis added). And perhaps the best way to end this discussion is to look at the words of Scripture that follow in Romans 10: 8-13; the italicized portions are of special relevance to this subject. May God bless you as you give your life freely to Him.

> But what saith it? The word is nigh thee, even in thy mouth, and in thy heart: that is, the word of faith, which we preach; That *if thou shalt confess* with thy mouth the Lord Jesus, *and shalt believe* in thine heart that God hath raised him from the dead, *thou shalt be saved.* For with the heart man *believeth unto righteousness*; and with the mouth *confession is made unto salvation.* For the scripture saith, *Whosoever believeth* on him *shall not be ashamed.* For there is no difference between the Jew and the Greek: for the same Lord *over all* is rich unto *all that call upon him.* For *whosoever* shall call upon the name of the Lord *shall be saved.* (emphasis added)

While this chapter is intended to bring clarity to the Potter in Romans 9, it is not exhaustive in dealing with the entire chapter. Romans 9:11-18 is also confusing to many in stating that God will have "mercy on whom he will have mercy" (v. 18). For an excellent explanation of this passage (as well as more on the Potter), I highly recommend a video presentation on this subject by the late pastor Adrian Rogers.[1]

Also, whether you are new to the subject of Calvinism or are working through its teachings, Bob Kirkland's book *Calvinism: None Dare Call It Heresy* is an excellent resource that is available through Lighthouse Trails as is Dave Hunt's book, *T.U.L.I.P. and the Bible.*

Chapter 9

Legalism or License Versus the Treasure of Living Water

> As the hart panteth after the water brooks, so panteth my soul after thee, O God. (Psalm 42:1)

Since 2002, Lighthouse Trails editors have conversed, either through e-mail, mail, or phone, with thousands of people. A good number of these people have come out of churches whose pastors and leaders have been trained in the seminaries and Christian colleges, which have, in large part, become havens for unbiblical teachings. These ill-equipped, misled pastors have brought their unscriptural teachings with them to the churches. We have heard the stories from so many of our readers of Christians they know who became caught under the bondage of legalism and then went to the opposite pole of turning grace into a license for sin. Many times when this happened, these confused Christians became involved with a dangerous mystical practice called contemplative prayer and joined emerging churches, thinking esoteric experiences and "new" freedoms were from God, especially when they compared them to their legalistic backgrounds.

It is this issue we desire to address in this chapter, with the hopes it may draw some back to the true living water that only Jesus Christ can give. Perhaps these words can alleviate some confusion to those who are held in bondage by either of these extremes.

In previous writings, we have demonstrated how the Gospel is the greatest of all treasures. Throughout the ages, man has been out digging for treasure. From the earth, we have been able to extract many of the things that we prize most highly including silver, gold, diamonds, gems, metal ores for making innumerable things made of iron or steel, copper or brass, and aluminum, while massive amounts of oil and coal have been extracted propelling us into an industrialized world. Yet, the human heart remains empty, and only God can fill that void.

Scripture likens our need for the Gospel to our need for water. Water is actually the most precious commodity on the planet. But most of us, if we have plenty of it, take it for granted. When scarce, it can be a matter of life and death. Water is life-giving, as we could only survive without it for a few days. So, in one sense, it is a priceless treasure; yet, in another sense, it is free. All this makes water a very suitable illustration for the Gospel because the Gospel is priceless in value, though it comes freely from the hand of God. Isaiah spoke of the Gospel and that it is both priceless and free. Consider his plea to his people to receive the gift of salvation:

> Ho, every one that thirsteth, come ye to the waters, and he that hath no money; come ye, buy, and eat; yea, come, buy wine and milk without money and without price. Wherefore do ye spend money for that which is not bread? and your labour for that which satisfieth not? hearken diligently unto me, and eat ye that which is good, and let your soul delight itself in fatness. Incline your ear, and come unto me: hear, and your soul shall live; and I will make an everlasting covenant with you, even the sure mercies of David. (Isaiah 55:1-3)

Already, in previous chapters of the book of Isaiah, he shared details of Jesus' suffering and consequent death on a cross as an atonement for sin (see especially Isaiah chapter 53). Jesus paid the price for

Legalism or License Versus the Treasure of Living Water

all our sins so that all who believe and put their trust in Him may go free and partake of the "sure mercies of David." The psalmist wrote:

> As the hart panteth after the water brooks, so panteth my soul after thee, O God. (Psalm 42:1)

And just as a deer is driven by thirst to drink of the cool water brooks, so we, like the psalmist, should hunger and thirst after God. But so many Christians today, especially those in the Western world, seek to quench that thirst in all the wrong places, and what they attain never really satisfies because it is *not* the living water that is able to give us life and renew us.

The Gospel has been with us for a very long time, but of the world's population, relatively few have chosen to dip into that water of life. The Scripture beckons:

> [T]he Spirit and the bride say, Come. And let him that heareth say, Come. And let him that is athirst come. And whosoever will, let him take the water of life freely. (Revelation 22:17)

Though the offer is made to all, there are so few who seem to listen. Consequently, so many choose to live in a perpetual drought, fearing the water of life that is able to save men's souls.

Now, how long has the Gospel been with us? Paul tells us that Abraham received the Gospel:

> And the scripture, forseeing that God would justify the heathen through faith, preached before the gospel unto Abraham, saying, In thee shall all nations be blessed. (Galatians 3:8)

God made a covenant with Abraham based on a promise to send a "seed" (namely Christ), and in that seed, the promises would be fulfilled (see Galatians 3:16). It is here that a date is given of four hundred thirty years before God gave the Law to Moses. And while the date is of no real significance, what *is* significant is that the New Covenant (the Gospel) came before the Old Covenant (the Law). Paul's letter to the Galatians vividly portrays how the Law was never given to save anyone; rather it was given to lead us to the Savior:

> Wherefore the law was our schoolmaster to bring us unto Christ, that we might be justified by faith. (Galatians 3:24)

The Law, a Way of Salvation?

Abraham was justified by faith and faith alone as Paul recounts that "Abraham believed God, and it was accounted to him for righteousness" (Galatians 3:6). Paul then emphatically states that no one is justified by the Law when he says, "But that no man is justified by the law in the sight of God, it is evident: for, *The just shall live by faith*" (Galatians 3:11, emphasis added). In fact, the Law was an impossible system for salvation because to break any of it even only once meant to break the whole Law:

> For as many as are of the works of the law are under the curse: for it is written, Cursed is every one that continueth not in all things which are written in the book of the law to do them. (Galatians 3:10)

James reiterates the power of the Law when he states:

> For whosoever shall keep the whole law, and yet offend in one point, he is guilty of all. (James 2:10)

It is clear, therefore, that the Law has power but not the power to save—unless, of course, a person keeps all the Law, at every point, perfectly; and no one has ever done that (except Jesus Christ). The power of the Law is to show us that because of sin, our righteousness is as filthy rags and consequently we remain under the curse of the Law until we come to Christ. The Law demonstrates that, without question, we are in need of a Redeemer; and that is why in Old Testament Law, lambs and bullocks were sacrificed year after year, not because they saved at all but because they served as a continual reminder of the need of a Savior who was to come. Even though the temple sacrifices were done at God's command, they could never in themselves take away sin because they were only symbols of what was to come (i.e., Jesus' sacrifice at Calvary). Chapter ten of Hebrews expounds on this point, as we look at the following:

> For the law having a shadow of good things to come, and not the very image of the things, can never with those sacrifices which they offered year by year continually make the comers thereunto perfect. For then would they not have ceased to be offered? because that the worshippers once purged should have had no more conscience of sins. But in those sacrifices there is a remembrance again made of sins every year. For it is not possible that the blood of bulls and of goats should take away sins. (Hebrews 10:1-4)

> And every priest standeth daily ministering and offering oftentimes the same sacrifices, which can never take away sins: But this man, after he had offered one sacrifice for sins for ever, sat down on the right hand of God. (Hebrews 10:11-12)

One teaching that is spread today is that the Jews are exempt from the Gospel because God gave them the Old Testament. But if that were true Paul would not have written "no man is justified by the law in the sight of God" (Galatians 3:11). On the contrary, it was to the Jews first that the apostles preached the Gospel until later when God showed them it was to be preached to the Gentiles also. The Gospel is for all people everywhere, Jew or Gentile. This is why the proclamation of the Gospel is so very important because, under God's plan, the way of salvation comes in only one way.

> For if the inheritance be of the law, it is no more of promise: but God gave it to Abraham by promise. (Galatians 3:18)

And when we think about it, the religions of the world believe we can be saved by our own goodness or that we already have God's divinity within and consequently have no need of a Savior. But God chose to show Abraham a different way, and all who come to God must come to Him in the same way:

> As for me, behold, my covenant is with thee, and thou shalt be a father of many nations. (Genesis 17:4)

So, when God made Abraham a father of many nations, He made it clear that this covenant, based on faith in a promise (i.e., Christ the Redeemer), was to be available to all people everywhere. Then came the Law four hundred and thirty years later to direct everyone, like a schoolmaster, to their need of a Redeemer as it exposes our sinfulness. In this sense, the Law can be likened to the test equipment in a doctor's office. After performing various tests, the doctor is able to identify a particular ailment, but the tests themselves have only exposed the problem and done nothing to render the cure. The doctor can then prescribe the proper medicine or refer the patient to a surgeon. Once that prescription or surgeon's referral has been made, the patient is bound rather than cured by his doctor's orders until the proper steps have been taken. Likewise, we remain bound under the curse of the Law until we come to Christ. Then He, as the Great Physician, cleanses us from our sin and imparts new life in us. That is why the Scripture says:

> Therefore if any man be in Christ, he is a new creature: old things are passed away; behold, all things are become new. (2 Corinthians 5:17)

Legalism or License Versus the Treasure of Living Water

This is also why Jesus said to the Samaritan woman at the well:

> Whosoever drinketh of this water shall thirst again: But whosoever drinketh of the water that I shall give him shall never thirst; but the water that I shall give him shall be in him a well of water springing up into everlasting life. (John 4:13-14)

This woman was acquainted with the problem, but now she had found the cure.

Likewise, Jesus' offer of "living water" (John 4:10) goes out to all people with the Holy Spirit's call, "whosoever will, let him take the water of life freely" (Revelation 22:17). I find it rather puzzling, though, that while countless numbers from all over the world have found that living water, many have the tendency to go back to the Law to find comfort and assurance there. Like the patient who is now cured but feels compelled to stay indefinitely in the doctor's office or the hospital when all that doctor can really do is to test and prescribe, if the Great Physician has already cured us, why would we want to go back into the Law that was designed to diagnose but not to cure? Furthermore, the Law can never be fulfilled by adherence to a set of rules; that is why Paul said:

> Love worketh no ill to his neighbour: therefore love is the fulfilling of the law. (Romans 13:10)

Somehow, we get to thinking that mechanically observing a set of rules pleases God, but God is concerned with the condition of our hearts. So, while we can fulfill the Law by love, we cannot do it by merely observing a set of rules. Like the patient holding onto the prescription, the Law is for those bound by sin, directing them to the Savior. The Law is good insomuch as it exposes our sin and brings us to our Savior, but it has no power to save. This is why Paul was so startled in hearing that the Galatians were going back into the Law and why he was compelled to write:

O foolish Galatians, who hath bewitched you, that ye should not obey the truth, before whose eyes Jesus Christ hath been evidently set forth, crucified among you? This only would I learn of you, Received ye the Spirit by the works of the law, or by the hearing of faith? Are ye so foolish? having begun in the Spirit, are ye now made perfect by the flesh? (Galatians 3:1-3)

Now, a License to Sin?

As I mentioned in the beginning of this chapter, many Christians who were raised in legalism, at some point, swung like a pendulum to the opposite extreme and began embracing not only a license to sin but also an entirely so-called "progressive" or emergent view of Christianity.[1] Instead of clinging to a set of legalistic rules that, they were told, are necessary to "complete" their salvation, they now adhere to a *new* set of rules that basically say there are *no* rules. In other words, all will be saved regardless of what they believe; and it doesn't really matter what a person does or how he lives—as long as he "has a good heart" and loves everyone. And now the Bible becomes an archaic book that might have some nice poetry in it, but it is no longer considered the inerrant word of God that we use as a guide to our spiritual lives.

Many who were raised in legalism and then made the leap to the opposite side of the spectrum have never actually tasted or taken a drink of the living water offered by Christ. In their effort to correct an erroneous system, they missed that which gives life altogether, not realizing that where they landed is just as much a life-killer as that from which they fled.

That Well of Living Water

Contrary to what many might teach, Paul was not offering the Galatians a license to sin but a fundamental truth of Scripture—that the Christian life can only be lived out as that well of living

Legalism or License Versus the Treasure of Living Water

water springs up from our hearts. It is imperative, therefore, that we be found in Christ because Jesus alone is that well from which the springs of life flow. The theologian and preacher Harry Ironside explains that well of living water that we so desperately need like this:

> A great many people make the mistake of trying to live the life before they receive the life. The hardest thing I know is to try to live the Christian life when you do not have it to live. There must be a Christian life first before you can exemplify and manifest it. To try to live a Christian life when you have never been born again is just as hopeless as for a chimpanzee to try and live a human life. I have seen some chimpanzees that could copy things people do in a remarkable way. At a zoo in Philadelphia, one of the worker's once said to me, "Come along and see a couple of your ancestors." I went along; there were two trained chimpanzees who had learned to mimic human beings to a remarkable degree. They wore clothes, sat at a table, ate, and drank, and in a clumsy way handled a knife and fork. When they got all through, they settled back and put cigarettes in their mouths, and a keeper lit them, and they looked to me exactly like a lot of our own people do when smoking cigarettes. I never was in such difficulty in assuring myself that there is no truth in evolution.
>
> Although those chimps could do all those things, they did not know anything about real human life. They did not know

anything of the principles controlling men and women. They were simply imitators. Many people imitate Christians and try to behave like them. They do not know anything of the power of the Christian life. They have never been born again. Jesus said, "Except a man be born again, he cannot see the Kingdom of God" (John 3:3).

Some people are seeking holiness of life when they need to be born again. They have joined the church; they have observed certain ordinances. They hear people talk of a deeper, more wonderful life, and they say, "That is what I want. I must go on and get into this richer, more blessed life." They try and try, and never get anywhere, because they have never begun right. They did not get in by the wicket gate.

You remember in John Bunyan's immortal allegory how Christian is going along a road, and a couple of fellows come jumping over the wall. "Who are you, and where do you come from," he asked.

"We come from the town of Carnal Security," they say to him. "We are going to the Celestial City."

"Well, you didn't get in where I did," says Christian in surprise, "I got in at the wicket gate."

"Oh, that is the old-fashioned way," they reply, "we have a short cut over the wall. After we are over the wall, what difference does it make? You are in the way, and we are in the way, and we are all headed for the same place. You'll see we will come out just as well as you."

But they didn't have the seal on their forehead. They had never been to the Cross; they did not have the robe of righteousness. You remember one fell over the cliff, and the other was lost in the forest. They never made their way to the Celestial City.

A lot of people get over the wall and not in by the wicket gate; never born again, they go striving for holiness, purity, and higher life, but it will be all in vain until they confess their sins in the presence of God and trust the Savior for themselves. They must give up all hope of righteousness in themselves, of being able to do anything to retrieve their condition, casting themselves wholly on Divine mercy. Then they are in the way and can grow in grace.[2]

Jesus Christ is the well of living water, offered freely to whosoever will invite Him into his life and heart to become his Savior. To the unbeliever, He is the invitation—"let him that is athirst come" (Revelation 22:17). To the new believer, He is that new life where, "old things are passed away; behold, all things are become new" (2 Corinthians 5:17). But to those who have known Christ for a while, even a long while, He is the reminder to come back and be refreshed again with the only water that "shall be in him a well of water springing up into everlasting life" (John 4:14).

Whether you have been caught in the vast sea of legalism or in the tsunami of "progressive" Christianity and you find your Christian life has become meaningless, tiresome, and without any real direction, why not come to the true living water? When we partake of that water, it does us much good. And when we share that water with others, it does no harm to our neighbor. It is the only water that is clean and pure and flows from the throne of God, and it is free for the taking.

Part III

A Faith Worth Believing

Till we all come in the unity of the faith, and of the knowledge of the Son of God, unto a perfect man, unto the measure of the stature of the fulness of Christ: That we henceforth be no more children, tossed to and fro, and carried about with every wind of doctrine, by the sleight of men, and cunning craftiness, whereby they lie in wait to deceive; But speaking the truth in love, may grow up into him in all things, which is the head, even Christ. (Ephesians 4: 13-15)

Chapter 10

Hard Lessons in Discernment

People often wonder, whether they verbalize it or not, why Lighthouse Trails has taken on the task of "criticizing other ministries." After all, isn't unity the most important thing in all of Christianity?

In 2023, for example, our office received an e-mail from someone who was very upset over our critiques and concerns of the movie series, *The Chosen*. Below is a portion of the comments we received from this person:

> With all due respect, you're absolutely wrong, and bearing (in a documented way) false witness against a brother [Dallas Jenkins] and his ministry. Maybe check up on what the word says about those practices, eh? . . . [Lighthouse Trails] is an organization that fashions themselves after the Pharisees of scripture . . . and gatekeeping the faith. . . . It's sad but true that there will always be that percentage of Christians who relish judging others and being purveyors of gossip and false witness, and you've found purpose in providing them fodder for their sinful attitudes. For shame.

It is difficult to read such harsh criticism; but we also know we don't stand alone; many of our readers have been accused of ungodly behavior when expressing concerns over practices or teachings they felt were unbiblical and spiritually dangerous.

In chapter one of this book "My Journey Out of Catholicism," I explain how I was raised Catholic and found the Lord after being drafted and sent to Germany as the Vietnam War was just ending. During this era, many young people in the '60s and '70s found the Lord as the Gospel was presented to hearts that were searching and hungry for truth. After my military duty ended, and I returned home (now as a born-again believer), I first got involved with a group in the Catholic charismatic movement. One of the great ironies of my Christian walk is that it was the charismatic Catholics who told me I had a "gift of discernment." I say ironic because it was discernment that led me out of the Catholic Church. As difficult as that time period was, it was also somewhat amusing that the spiritual gift the Catholic charismatics said I had was actually rejected by them as I began questioning practices like "inner healing," contemplative prayer, "slaying in the Spirit," and deliverance rituals.

Lessons in Harsh Criticisms

Over the years since then, I've given a lot of thought to what biblical discernment is all about and have come to realize it's so important to be sensitive to what the Lord wants us to do as a ministry. For one, we know we can't cover every topic, so we seek the Lord on what He would have us to do.

This may come as a surprise, but some of the harshest criticisms we've ever received were not about exposing error in the church but that we weren't doing enough. In at least two cases, the offended party told us they would do all they could do to destroy Lighthouse Trails and the ministries of some of our authors because we would not post or cover an issue they felt we should cover. At this point, their initial request that we would post *their* material now became a demand!

The argument in each case was basically that because we would not expose a particular person or error, we must be in league with the enemy, and consequently, heretics and deceivers. These threats were brutal in that these parties said they would use whatever means or media they could avail themselves with to destroy Lighthouse Trails. As far as handling such situations, we made the decision many years ago that if an attack was unwarranted, rather than quickly coming to our own defense, we would lean on the Lord's protection and trust Him to vindicate us as He saw fit.

There were a few reasons why we refused to post these materials on our website: first and foremost, we wanted to be led by the Lord and not by intimidation and threats; second, in these severe cases and in others as well, the materials being presented to us were vehement, poorly researched, and even slanderous and erroneous. Lighthouse Trails has always tried to be careful in our treatment of those who bring false teachings into the church. As much as we can, we try to keep our focus on the false teachings themselves with the hopes that these false teachings might cease—or at least be exposed and avoided. We realize it is not our job or even within our ability to know the heart and motives of those presenting false teachings. But, at the same time, we are not naïve enough as to not see the apostasy that is presently sweeping our world and the church.

One of these individuals who said he would destroy Lighthouse Trails (largely because we wouldn't post his materials) said that when he exposes someone, he likes to go for the "shock and the awe" as he attempts to destroy someone's reputation. As we see it, such an attitude goes against the purpose of a biblical discernment ministry, which is to aid and serve the body of Christ by exposing things that are a dangerous hindrance to finding or walking with God and exhorting the church to remain anchored to the truth found in God's Word.

The Chosen: An Unpleasant Task in Discernment

In First John chapter 4, John distinguishes the spirit of antichrist from the true Christ by using the Gospel itself as the standard for measurement. I have written about this before: It is the idea that anything that tears down the Gospel is not of God, and whatever builds it up is of God. This standard has also been the tool we employ in deciding what subjects to write about. You see, the Gospel has everything to do with our eternal destiny, so it is essential that we defend and protect it. It's important to remember too that the spirit of antichrist is not always portrayed as hatred of Christ, but it can often come in a much more subtle form as a substitute for Christ or an imitation (i.e., false) Christ.

In this chapter about difficult lessons in discernment, I decided to use *The Chosen* as an example. What I said in the previous paragraph is why we took on warning about it. Doing this has not been a pleasant task; we already had friends, family members, and readers who felt, at first, that *The Chosen* was a wonderful way of presenting the Gospel, and after all, Christian leaders are recommending it.

> Something was amiss; it became apparent that a dismantling of the Gospel was taking place where Jesus, the Son of God, takes on more and more human qualities to the point that He is just like us.

But something was amiss; and as we did our research, it became apparent that a subtle (and sometimes not so subtle) dismantling of the Gospel was taking place where Jesus, the Son of God, takes on more and more human qualities to the point that He is just like us. Now, it may seem OK to some to do this since the Gospel teaches us that Jesus is fully

Hard Lessons in Discernment

God and fully man; but what happens when we see, on the screen, that Jesus is just another one of us? What happens when we see one of Jesus' disciples helping Him recite His lines for His sermon on the Mount? And what will happen to Derral Eves' (*The Chosen's* Mormon CEO and Executive Producer) teenage son, who rushed to his father in the middle of the night with joyful tears in his eyes, saying "Dad, Jesus really does live, doesn't he . . . and he's a real person, right?" His son said this after viewing a scene in *The Chosen* in season three where "Jesus" was "blowing raspberries" (i.e., making flatulence sounds with his lips) while interacting among children.[1]

This scene was obviously intended to be funny, but it was clearly an attempt to bring Jesus down to our level which very much lines up with Mormonism (which teaches that Jesus was just a man who *attained* divinity, just as Mormon believers will attain godhood). As we learn more about Mormonism, we find that "Heaven" will be a place where Joseph Smith will be seated next to the Father (in as much prominence as Jesus Christ), and Jesus will be further removed sitting among various historical figures.

Then consider John the Baptist who is depicted in *The Chosen* as "creepy John."[2] At face value, John could have been seen as creepy to his culture; after all, he was out there in the desert eating locusts and honey. But if we search the Scriptures to see what John was really like and how people perceived him, to call him "creepy John" is not "plausible"[3] as Dallas Jenkins likes to call his version of Bible stories—it is fabrication and slanderous!

As it turns out, John was loved and respected by many—both Jew and Gentile. More importantly, we should note how God perceived him. In Luke, chapter one, an angel spoke these words about John:

> For he shall be great in the sight of the Lord, and shall drink neither wine nor strong drink; and he shall be filled with the Holy Ghost, even from his mother's womb. . . . And he shall go before him in the spirit and power of Elias, to turn the hearts of the fathers to the children, and

the disobedient to the wisdom of the just; to make ready a people prepared for the Lord. (Luke 1:15, 17)

Then in Luke chapter 7, Jesus spoke of John's ministry as very honorable saying, "Among those that are born of women there is not a greater prophet than John the Baptist" (Luke 7:28). With these verses in mind, it is puzzling, then, that *The Chosen* would depict "creepy John" as someone Jesus felt was going off the deep end and needing correction.[4]

Reading further in Luke 7, and in light of the depiction of John in *The Chosen*, it is amazing to see what Jesus said next because, while multitudes of people went to hear and be baptized by John, a small minority would not hear him, and these were "the Pharisees and lawyers [who] rejected the counsel of God against themselves, being not baptized of him" (Luke 7:30). What caught my attention first in this Bible passage is the fact that Jesus addresses the Pharisees and describes what they are like; so I was curious to see what Jesus had to say about them, having been freshly accused of being modern-day Pharisees ourselves. Speaking of these men, Jesus said:

> Whereunto then shall I liken the men of this generation? and to what are they like? They are like unto children sitting in the marketplace, and calling one to another, and saying, We have piped unto you, and ye have not danced; we have mourned to you, and ye have not wept. For John the Baptist came neither eating bread nor drinking wine; and ye say, He hath a devil. The Son of man is come eating and drinking; and ye say, Behold a gluttonous man, and a winebibber, a friend of publicans and sinners! (Luke 7:31-34)

Now, let's be careful here in understanding what Jesus is trying to say: Jesus is not authenticating the view that Jesus (or His disciples) are party animals who go out and get drunk, nor is He authenticating the view that John the Baptist is creepy or mad or "hath a devil." No actually, He is denying it.

Reading these verses reminded me again about *The Chosen* episode where Jesus has a disciple help recite His lines for the Sermon on the Mount. In Scripture, did Jesus have something to say on that subject? Let's consider the following words of Jesus:

> Then said Jesus unto them, When ye have lifted up the Son of man, then shall ye know that I am he, and that I do nothing of myself; but as my Father hath taught me, I speak these things. (John 8:28)

Does this sound like Jesus practiced His lines with the help of a disciple, where in fact, He only wanted to speak what He received of the Father? Jesus spoke the things He received directly from the Father because Jesus was eternally God with the Father. And He is telling the people here that when they see Him crucified, die, and rise again, they will know who was with them. Again, we see a gradual whittling down of Jesus in *The Chosen* to being just a man. Dallas Jenkins claims to be presenting the "authentic Jesus"[5] in this series while only using five percent of Scripture.[6] It seems more like they are trying to present an authentic Jesus while contradicting Scripture (something impossible to do!). Again, the die has been cast, and it appears that the Jesus of *The Chosen* resembles more that of the Book of Mormon than that of Holy Scripture.

A Lesson in Finding the Truth: *The Chosen* and the Mormons

Given that the Mormon producers of *The Chosen* are obligated by their religion to stay true to the Book of Mormon, how can they justify depicting Jesus as revealed in the Holy Bible when their Book of Mormon supersedes the Bible? This is a real predicament as the Mormons have invested heavily into this production.

Perhaps for a time, it will be possible to ride the neutrality, but the day will surely come when they will have to abide by their true persuasions. Most likely, by then, the damage will already be done in gradually sizing Jesus down to just a man who *eventually* became "god" just as all Mormons will one day become gods—that is, as the Book of Mormon teaches.

A while back, Dallas Jenkins made a statement indicating it is OK to have Mormons involved in the creation of *The Chosen* series, by saying that Mormons and Christians believe in the same Jesus.[7] What he should have said is Christianity and Mormonism have entirely separate views of who Jesus was and who He is. Jesus, according to Mormonism, was never part of the eternal Godhead but *attained* godhood just as they believe man can attain godhood. Consequently, Jesus can never become one's Savior under that belief system.

What we see happening in *The Chosen* series is a subtle and gradual dismantling of Jesus Christ, the disciples, and the Bible itself. This is serious because, while this series may be entertaining, the distortions to Scripture can have eternal consequences. Some argue that *The Chosen* will stimulate people to read their Bibles; but just like the Book of Mormon, this series may easily supplant the Bible (and probably already has because of its powerful seduction of the senses), and it will be the only "Bible" many viewers will ever know. We have already seen this happen with *Jesus Calling*, where readers of this book contacted us to admit that they had become so "addicted" to and enamored with the romantic nature of this "Jesus" that they increasingly set their Bibles aside and used this book for their devotional reading.

A Lesson in Knowing Who We Are and Who He Is

In closing this chapter, I would like to make a few remarks about distinguishing truth from error. First, in referring back to the e-mail we received from our critic who parenthetically injected a keen observation about our position on *The Chosen*, I am very thankful. She said we present our information "in a documented way," which, in and of itself, is a compliment. We research things carefully to get to the truth on any issue. For example, when we said that only five percent of *The Chosen* is from the Bible, we were quoting Dallas Jenkins himself who said this. The point is, it's valuable to do the research though it takes much time and effort before making an observation or a criticism. Another point she made was in referring to us as gatekeepers of the faith, but that is something we have neither earned nor deserved. Jesus is the sheepgate. He stated that when He said:

> I am the door: by me if any man enter in, he shall be saved, and shall go in and out, and find pasture. (John 10:9)

By this, Jesus was indicating that He is our all in all things. Paul expanded on the various aspects of what Jesus does for us when he said:

> But of him are ye in Christ Jesus, who of God is made unto us wisdom, and righteousness, and sanctification, and redemption. (1 Corinthians 1:30)

In other words, Jesus provides everything we need for salvation and Christian living. Indeed, He is both the gate and the gatekeeper of our faith, enabling us to discern what is good and what is not.

> **Jesus is both the gate and the gatekeeper of our faith, enabling us to discern what is good and what is not.**

There will come a time when we will meet the Lord, and there will be plenty of surprises when God reveals how much that was done "for God" was actually counter-productive. May we humbly seek Him to help us to build His kingdom and not tear it down. On that day, God will test our lives (and ministries) as with fire to a house—some built with straw and some built with stone.

I find myself described in the same chapter from Paul when he says:

> For ye see your calling, brethren, how that not many wise men after the flesh, not many mighty, not many noble, are called: But God hath chosen *the foolish things of the world* to confound the wise; and God hath chosen *the weak things of the world* to confound the things which are mighty; And *base things of the world,* and *things which are despised,* hath God chosen, yea, and *things which are not,* to bring to nought things that are: That no flesh should glory in his presence. But of him are ye in Christ Jesus, who of God is made unto us wisdom, and righteousness, and sanctification, and redemption: That, according as it is written, He that glorieth, let him glory in the Lord. (1 Corinthians 1: 26-31; emphasis added)

Do you find yourself described in these verses? If so, you are in good company, and God can use you even through the hardest lessons of discernment.

Chapter 11

A Master Carpenter Builds His Church

Looking for a Carpenter

In this chapter, I would like to take you on a historical journey into the past through the record of Scripture. History books inadvertently have a certain level of bias, but the Bible is not so, for it is inspired of God and consequently totally accurate. We will also take a glimpse into the future through the prophetic eye of Scripture. Again, the Bible has and will continue to always be one hundred percent accurate. With this kind of accuracy, we have a decisive means with which to steer our course and to get a sense of where we are.

We begin our search into the past by looking for a carpenter. If we can get a hold of a certain carpenter, he can tell us what's wrong with the church. You see, much of the church of today is rickety and on the brink of collapse. Some of the churches may seem just fine. Their attendance may number a thousand or more, and their income makes elaborate expansion possible. Don't get me wrong; in and of itself, there is nothing wrong with a church having good attendance and a self-sustaining income, but that is not what forms a good church. We must look beneath the outer surface and see what is being used for the foundation of the church. Then, too, we will want to see what kinds of materials are being used to build upon the foundation. If the foundation is good and the materials are good, we can expect to have a strong church.

Unfortunately, over the years, our ministry has been contacted by various ministers (holding high credentials) who told us we at Lighthouse Trails are not qualified to discern. I was always surprised when this happened because I did not know that discernment had a qualification. In fact, I have known uneducated people who evidence more discernment than some of these professors and leaders. Be that as it may, we humbly remit that we do not have the credentials they are looking for. And, hence, we are out, looking for a carpenter.

Finding a Master Carpenter

In seeking this particular carpenter, we've moved back now to more than 2000 years ago to a stable in a small city because we are told that the redeemer of all people of all nations was born in Bethlehem.

> But thou, Bethlehem Ephratah, though thou be little among the thousands of Judah, yet out of thee shall he come forth unto me that is to be ruler in Israel; whose goings forth have been from of old, from everlasting. (Micah 5:2)

Little is said in the New Testament of the years preceding Jesus' public ministry, but we know He was the son of Joseph, a carpenter, and hence became a carpenter Himself. And while we know little of the early years, His life and teachings reflect His skill as a master carpenter.

The word *carpenter* is only used twice in the entire New Testament, yet in both cases, it is in reference to Jesus:

A Master Carpenter and His Church

> Is not this *the carpenter's son*? is not his mother called Mary? and his brethren, James, and Joses, and Simon, and Judas? And his sisters, are they not all with us? Whence then hath this man all these things? And they were offended in him. (Matthew 13:55-57; emphasis added)

> Is not this *the carpenter,* the son of Mary, the brother of James, and Joses, and of Juda, and Simon? and are not his sisters here with us? And they were offended at him. But Jesus said unto them, A prophet is not without honour, but in his own country, and among his own kin, and in his own house. And he could there do no mighty work, save that he laid his hands upon a few sick folk, and healed them. And he marvelled because of their unbelief. And he went round about the villages, teaching. (Mark 6:3-6; emphasis added)

From these two passages, we can extract bits of information. From the first, we see that Jesus was known as "the carpenter's son" while the second passage identifies Him as "the carpenter." After Jesus began His public ministry, the religious leaders were seething with jealousy because they lacked the depth of wisdom, understanding, and spiritual power that Jesus had without their formal education. Instead of drawing near to glean and learn from Him, they separated themselves from Him. Can you imagine the opportunities they missed by withdrawing from our very Savior? His siblings, too, apparently did not recognize Him as suggested by Jesus' statement that a prophet is not recognized even in his own house (Mark 6:4). Some speculate that James, who became the highest authority in deciding matters of doctrine in the early church (see Acts 15:13-21), was so humbled and ashamed for not recognizing Jesus while He lived, that he ascribed to himself no special recognition or honors when he wrote his epistle other than beginning with the words, "James, a servant of God and of the Lord Jesus Christ" (James 1:1).

It is also unfortunate that this period of Jesus' history has often been obscured or even twisted to accommodate various points of view. For example, Catholic theologians insist that Jesus had no brothers or sisters; otherwise, this would impede on their view that Mary, as the "mother of God," had to be both sinless and a perpetual virgin. Ellen G. White (founder of the Seventh Day Adventists), on the other hand, insisted that Jesus had *older* brothers; but this idea negates the possibility of Jesus being born to a virgin, which view is totally faulty as well. It is important, then, that we be like the citizens of Berea who "received the word with all readiness of mind, and searched the scriptures daily, whether those things were so" (Acts 17:11).

Thus far, we have established that Jesus was born to a carpenter and became a carpenter Himself—most likely with carpentry being a family business. We should, therefore, take a moment to examine what it meant to be a carpenter in Jesus' day. According to *Strong's Concordance*, the Greek word for carpenter, found only twice in the New Testament, is *tekton* (meaning "a craftsman in wood"—see Greek entry #5045). It's interesting that this word is only used in the New Testament to describe Jesus. He was a skilled craftsman who probably started young and had many years of experience. He perhaps had a shop from which He and His father and younger brothers worked. So, while we can expect that this family business was likely involved in building construction and home repairs, much of the work was probably done right at the shop to do any variety of wood projects.

The Carpenter Shows the Way

One such project Jesus and His father, Joseph, must have been familiar with is the construction of wooden yokes for beasts of burden. Consider, for example, the following plea spoken by Jesus during His public ministry:

> Come unto me, all ye that labour and are heavy laden, and I will give you rest. Take my yoke upon you, and learn of me; for I am meek and lowly in heart: and ye shall find rest unto your souls. For my yoke is easy, and my burden is light. (Matthew 11:28-30)

As a carpenter, Jesus would have known how to fashion a yoke that fit a working animal well. But He also knew what yoke the Jewish people were under in that day. In addition to their burden of being under Roman occupation, their own religious leaders had taken the Mosaic Law and added so many stipulations that the Jewish people were scarcely able to budge from their requirements for living a "good" life. Jesus addressed these leaders in open rebuke by saying:

> But woe unto you, scribes and Pharisees, hypocrites! for ye shut up the kingdom of heaven against men: for ye neither go in yourselves, neither suffer ye them that are entering to go in. (Matthew 23:13)

After describing the yoke the leaders had placed on their followers, Jesus said:

> For they bind heavy burdens and grievous to be borne, and lay them on men's shoulders; but they themselves will not move them with one of their fingers. (Matthew 23:4)

Jesus also knew that no one could gain eternal life by means of observing the laws of Moses because the Law has never been kept perfectly by anyone (except Jesus), and therefore everyone needs a redeemer. The Old Covenant thus exposes our sin and shows us only that we are in a lost condition. The New Covenant that Jesus sealed with His own blood gives us eternal life.

So when the Jewish people asked Jesus what work they must perform to gain eternal life, He merely said, "This is the work of God, that ye believe on him whom he hath sent" (John 6:29).

Jesus made the way to eternal life accessible to all. His only requirement is that we believe the Gospel. This is the yoke to which He was referring when He said, "my yoke is easy." It is also the plan of salvation Isaiah spoke of when he wrote:

> And an highway shall be there, and a way, and it shall be called The way of holiness; the unclean shall not pass over it; but it shall be for those: the wayfaring men, though fools, shall not err therein. (Isaiah 35:8)

There is only one way of holiness, and that is to have the righteousness of Christ imputed to us. When we put our faith in Christ alone for salvation, we apply the blood that was shed for all sinners—the blood that "cleanseth us from all sin" (1 John 1:7). When we place our faith in Christ, God also gives us a new birth whereby we become partakers of a new nature with a heart for good works.

The Carpenter and the Church

Now, we have established that Jesus is the carpenter for whom we are looking to examine the Christian church of today. After two thousand years, it is in need of repairs. But first, we must learn of Him what constitutes a strongly built church. So let us turn to Him now and hear what He has to say about building construction:

> Therefore whosoever heareth these sayings of mine, and doeth them, I will liken him unto a wise man, which built his house upon a rock: And the rain descended, and the floods came, and the winds blew, and beat upon that house; and it fell not: for it was founded upon a rock. And every one that heareth these sayings of mine, and doeth

them not, shall be likened unto a foolish man, which built his house upon the sand: And the rain descended, and the floods came, and the winds blew, and beat upon that house; and it fell: and great was the fall of it. (Matthew 7:24-27)

It is important, then, that the church be built upon solid rock in order to withstand the tests of time. The Greek word for "rock" used here is *petra* meaning "a mass of rock." To understand what Jesus is really talking about, let's look at His discourse with a man named Simon (later called Peter). When Jesus first met Simon, He gave him a surname:

And he brought him to Jesus. And when Jesus beheld him, he said, Thou art Simon the son of Jona: thou shalt be called Cephas, which is by interpretation, A stone. (John 1:42)

The name Cephas is found six times in the Bible, and each time it refers specifically to Peter. In a later discussion, Jesus asked His disciples "whom say ye that I am?" (Matthew 16:15) to which Simon Peter replied, "Thou art the Christ, the Son of the living God" (v. 16). In response to this, Jesus revealed the importance of what Simon Peter had said while giving him yet another new name:

And I say also unto thee, That thou art Peter [Petros], and upon this rock [petra] I will build my church; and the gates of hell shall not prevail against it. (v. 18)

It is here that Jesus reveals the secret to a healthy church. Notice that the word petra is used again as in the parable Jesus used earlier to describe the importance of building on solid rock. So when Jesus now says, "upon this rock I will build my church," He is not referring to Peter, a stone, but to the foundational truth Peter had just disclosed, namely that Jesus is truly "the Christ, the Son of the living God." True Christianity always was and always will be rooted in the Gospel. Scripture says, "If the foundations be destroyed, what can the righteous do?" (Psalm 11:3). This is as much of a statement as it is a question because it urges us to keep the foundation of our faith intact. Great harm has been inflicted on the church as New Age practices and beliefs and emergent-church ideologies have infiltrated the church with their toxic teachings that Jesus never really atoned for sin but was just a role model for "Christ" consciousness. As for Peter being our first pope with infallible qualities (which the Catholic Church teaches), Jesus made it clear this was not the case when only a few verses later He said to Peter, "Get thee behind me, Satan" (v. 23).

However, Jesus did leave Peter with a key—i.e., the Gospel and a place in the church as one of the building stones firmly planted on the significance of the Cross as the only way to Heaven. It should be noted that the term petra is never ascribed to Peter in the New Testament but is always used in reference to Jesus. Jesus is also referred to as the *chief* cornerstone and the "head of the corner" to show that only *He* has the critical and most significant place in the church.

In Acts 4, Peter spoke of the special place Jesus has as the foundation of the church:

> This is the stone which was set at nought of you builders, which is become the head of the corner. Neither is there salvation in any other: for there is none other name under heaven given among men, whereby we must be saved. (Acts 4:11-12)

Then, in 1 Peter 2, Peter alluded to the proper construction of the church. He refers to Jesus as the "chief corner stone" (v. 6) and "the head of the corner" (v. 7), but he also includes himself and *all* believers as "lively stones (*lithos*)" (v. 5). It is important to recognize what Peter *is* and *is not* saying in this chapter because he goes on to refer to all believers as "a royal priesthood" (v. 9). Peter never intended that he should be called "pope." Neither did he see a unique priesthood performing transubstantiation (i.e., the Catholic belief that priests can change the bread and wine into the actual body and blood of Christ) on an altar. Rather, he recognized the priesthood of all believers in that Jesus had already performed a one-time sacrifice that was perfect and complete (see Hebrews 9:24-28). Peter witnessed Christians throughout the community breaking bread daily as a remembrance of Jesus' death on the Cross for all sin. Nor did any of the apostles frown on this practice as something that only "priests" can and must do because in John 6, Jesus had already reprimanded them for even considering that partaking of the "bread of life" should be viewed as a literal eating of His flesh and blood (see vv. 61-63). Rather, Peter saw a vibrant church of "living stones" rejoicing in the salvation that Jesus brought to those who would believe on Him—a salvation that was and is perfect, complete, and for certain to "whosoever believeth." There is no fading with this covenant. Moses covered his face with a veil whereby the children of Israel could not see "the end of that which is abolished" (2 Corinthians 3:13), but the apostles had no need to cover their faces but rather proclaimed the unending glory of the New Covenant sealed in the blood of the perfect Lamb.

The Carpenter and the Purifying of the Church

God is not through with His church. Remember, Jesus promised Peter that the gates of Hell would not prevail against the church. Yet, to many of us, it appears that the church at large has entered an accelerated state of apostasy that is unsurmountable as more and more of it is succumbing to broad-sweeping interfaith ecumenism, New Age and esoteric experiences, and anti-biblical "social justice" beliefs. Even so, God's Word will not fail.

I believe we could be entering a special time when God is about to purify the church. While there is much talk and conjecture among many of today's most popular Christian leaders that a great revival and "awakening" is nearly upon us, the evidence of a mass true revival is not there. What *is* evident is a massive amount of apostasy. Yet, at the same time, from what we can see as we hear from believers all over the world, it seems God is separating and purifying genuine believers while calling those who are riding the fence of apostasy to come to the side of uncompromising faith in Jesus Christ—back to the Gospel, back to the foundation of our faith.

Back in the 1970s, when I was a new believer, I remember hearing an evangelist quoting from this verse in Ephesians:

> That he might present it to himself a glorious church, not having spot, or wrinkle, or any such thing; but that it should be holy and without blemish. (Ephesians 5:27).

He then looked up at his audience and said, "It looks like God has a lot of washing and ironing to do!" He said this during the "Jesus people" movement. Today, things have gotten so much worse. But, at the same time, I see a body of believers from all over the world holding to their convictions to stand on the side of truth and God's Word. What I see, however, is the unseen. It is a hidden body of believers who love the Lord with all their hearts and seek to serve Him, not with their own strength, but with His, of which He has promised to give those who follow Him.

A Carpenter Who Prepares Us for the Future

At the time I began working on this chapter (initially as an article), I had not yet heard of the coronavirus. In 2020, that is about the only thing one was hearing on the news. For many, it was a roller-coaster ride trying to decipher the seriousness and magnitude of this pandemic. Coming from two extremes, some tried to minimize what was happening by suggesting it was a hoax while others seemed to think this was the end of the world. Jesus spoke of a time when "the end is not by and by" (Luke 21:9) that will be marked by wars and commotions along with "great earthquakes . . . in divers places, and famines, and pestilences . . ." (v. 11). Jesus said when you witness these things, "be not terrified" (v. 9). While the coronavirus definitely seemed like one of the pestilences Jesus said would come, I also believe it was another wake-up call that God was using to get us ready to face the future. But how do we go about preparing for the future?

Many practical measures were being taken in dealing with the coronavirus, and I fully agree that practical measures need to be taken. Yet, as believers in Christ, we do not want to miss the spiritual significance of what is happening.

Looking back, we can see that Covid-19 ramped up talk by New Age and political globalist thinkers who say the world needs a new-world order. They even see Covid as a positive means to a desirable end—i.e., the merging and unity of all beliefs, all people, and all nations. We saw this happen to some degree with the aftermath of 9-11 where we witnessed a push for ecumenism (in the religious realm) and global unity. But very little actually happened in seeing a genuine effort at repentance and turning to God.

So during a virus crisis, let us do the practical things that need to be done, but let us more so, as those who understand the times in which we live from a biblical perspective, prepare for a change in the spiritual climate of our nation and the world where genuine Christians will be more ostracized, and one-world thinkers will be glorified. The truth is, the world will continue to witness more of the things Jesus described in Luke 21 as a result of the world not turning to God in sincere and humble repentance.

In seeking God for a word of encouragement for our readers, I found a very sure word of hope in the Scriptures that relates to both Covid and the present state of the church. In his second epistle, Peter writes:

> Whereby are given unto us exceeding great and precious promises: that by these ye might be partakers of the divine

nature, having escaped the corruption that is in the world through lust. (2 Peter 1:4)

> Jesus' promises that the gates of hell will not prevail against the church and that He is preparing for Himself "a glorious church, not having spot, or wrinkle."

Peter also says, in verse 19, "We have also a more sure word of prophecy." We can, therefore, find the encouragement we need in the Scriptures as we lay hold of God's promises and assurances for the future.

Thus, let us remind ourselves of Jesus' promise to Peter (and to us) that the gates of hell will not prevail against the church (Matthew 16:18) and that He is preparing for Himself "a glorious church, not having spot, or wrinkle" (Ephesians 5:27). Consider also the words of David to his son Solomon concerning the construction of Solomon's temple:

> And David said to Solomon his son, Be strong and of good courage, and do it: fear not, nor be dismayed: for the LORD God, even my God, will be with thee; he will not fail thee, nor forsake thee, until thou hast finished all the work for the service of the house of the LORD. (1 Chronicles 28:20)

These same words can be applicable to us today. Solomon's temple has come and gone, but God is not yet finished with building the invisible body of believers called "the church." In light of Jesus' promise to Peter, this verse takes on special significance in that it can assure us that God will accomplish all that He has set out for each of us to do as part of God's spiritual body.

Furthermore, it is such promises as these that can help us on the more personal level. All of us struggle, at one time or another, with the prospect of death, and the coronavirus caught everyone's attention on a global scale. But these fears can grab us at different levels. There is, of course, the prospect of facing our own death, and our concerns here can be multiplied if we have family or loved ones who need our help. Questions arise like, what will happen to them if I am gone? Then, too, there is the prospect of losing a loved one. Ordinarily, we do not like to think of such things because they are too painful—until something like a pandemic happens. Here, as well, we can look to the Scriptures for support, allowing the Holy Spirit (the Comforter) to speak to us through His Word.

The prophet Isaiah suffered much and witnessed a lot of calamity in his lifetime, but he also drew strength and comfort in knowing that God would not fail to accomplish His purposes though the world be torn apart. God is, and has always been, faithful as the book of Isaiah expresses so beautifully:

> For as the heavens are higher than the earth, so are my ways higher than your ways, and my thoughts than your thoughts. For as the rain cometh down, and the snow from heaven, and returneth not thither, but watereth the earth, and maketh it bring forth and bud, that it may give seed to the sower, and bread to the eater: So shall my word be that goeth forth out of my mouth: it shall not return unto me void, but it shall accomplish that which I please, and it shall prosper in the thing whereto I sent it. (Isaiah 55:9-11)

One of the greatest comforts we, as believers, can have is knowing and believing that God will fulfill all He has set out to do in our individual lives and in that glorious church He is building, and He has promised to never leave or forsake us. That master Carpenter will complete what He has set out to do.

> For ye shall go out with joy, and be led forth with peace: the mountains and the hills shall break forth before you into singing, and all the trees of the field shall clap their hands. (Isaiah 55:12)

Chapter 12

Preparing For Perilous Times and Finding God's Peace in the Midst of Them

Over the last several years since Lighthouse Trails began, we have been contacted by many who love the Lord and were struggling with great challenges. Some were ostracized by their churches that had gone Purpose Driven, contemplative, or emerging; some had division in their families; some had financial concerns; and others were worried about health issues—whether their own or those of loved ones. Beyond all this, many have expressed a sense of uncertainty or foreboding of what the future will bring.

The Bible indicates that in the last days perilous times shall come. As it has become increasingly obvious, by all indications, that America is racing toward judgment, so too is the realization that something serious or catastrophic could easily come to our country, and we are unprepared. Whether it be nuclear attack, economic collapse, or natural disasters, America appears to be getting only closer to that day.

I know that for the average American (including the American Christian) the idea that mighty America could stumble and fall simply does not register. After all, how could a loving God bring calamity on a nation that has stood so tall for so long? But in considering this, we can see it is not God who has rejected us but our nation that has continually rejected Him. A case in point is a pastor in a small Oregon town who shared with me how occasionally his church would be permitted to hold an assembly at the local public high school, but one day the mayor approached him and said, "If you even mention God at the assembly, I will have you out of here so fast . . ." But what is a pastor supposed to talk about if he cannot talk about God? Yet, what is even more grievous than our lost freedom is that so many churches have become apostate as they welcome immorality, mystical practices, and false doctrines while often viewing the atonement as outdated and dogmatic.

When Judgment Comes...

When judgment comes upon America, it will not be because of a hateful God entertaining Himself with calamity but rather because we, as a nation, have brought judgment upon ourselves. While this nation has a heritage of many who, through great personal sacrifice and a love for God, invited God into the affairs of our nation (and our nation has known prosperity and peace on all our borders) we forget that these blessings all came from God. Now that we have pushed God aside and booted Him out of the country, we have also booted out the blessings and protection we have long known.

None of us really knows what our nation will become if/when judgment befalls us, but frankly, I have a much more ominous feeling about how corrupt and lawless it will become if God does *not* judge us. While the call to repentance has been going out for decades now, things have clearly only gotten worse. And while many churches are mustering up for national "repentance" and "revival," God has already moved on to the next step. It is a true saying that those who have sown to the wind will only reap the whirlwind.

Unfortunately, there is much apathy when it comes to warnings of judgment or cataclysmic events. While many prosperity prophets tickle the ears of those who want a soft feel-good gospel, others, in contrast, give warnings of such horrendous proportions (even offering specific dates) of events that could annihilate vast portions of the planet; the net result is that many are being conditioned into indifference.

When perilous events come, be it judgment or persecution, will we as Christians be ready for it? Such changes can come very rapidly and seemingly overnight; Anita Dittman and Diet Eman (Lighthouse Trails' Holocaust-survivor authors) knew this was true and witnessed it firsthand. Jesus said that men's hearts will fail from fear of seeing the events happening around them (Luke 21:26). In Luke 21 and Matthew 24, Jesus gives a basic outline of the peril that will precede His return; He did not give specific calendar dates of what will happen, but He did teach us (as do the apostles and prophets) how we can be ready to face the future.

> When perilous events come, be it judgment or persecution, will we as Christians be ready for it? Such changes can come very rapidly and seemingly overnight.

I'm sure we have all seen the ill effects that fear and worry can have on a person's life, both spiritually and physically. Fear and worry, over an extended period of time, stagnates one spiritually, cripples one emotionally, and breaks one down physically. The enemy (Satan) uses fear whenever possible to thwart the progress of Christians and to promote his agenda. Whole societies have been controlled through fear. When we consider what happened in Nazi Germany, it's true that great numbers were mesmerized by a charismatic leader with a demonic anointing, but overall he was able to rule the country through fear. Today, we already see the reemergence of fear and intimidation both in our politics and in many churches where fundamental (i.e., biblical) Christianity is marginalized, if not villainized, while immorality and corruption are given special sanctions and promotion.

Being Prepared

How can a Christian believer stand under this kind of pressure we see today? Fear is already at work eroding the values we have long held sacred. In many churches, just the pressure to remain popular or contemporary is enough to introduce Yoga and mind-altering meditation (formerly called an occultic practice but today repackaged as "contemplative prayer" and Spiritual Formation) into our churches.

Will the Christians who are still holding back from this landslide of compromised Christianity eventually cower and be absorbed into the system? Will we, like Judas, proceed to give Jesus a kiss while undermining everything He taught? Or will we, like Peter, deny that we even knew Him? The fact is, Jesus is being betrayed and denied on a massive scale today by proclaiming Christians through their embracing of false teachings, false christs, and "another gospel" (2 Corinthians 11:4). We are seeing the worst kind of betrayal.

Fear is not something you can merely put the brakes on—like pressing a pedal in your car. Peter, who so adamantly insisted to Jesus that he would never deny Him even unto death, did so three times in the course of one night. How then does one stem the tide of fear (and worry) in his own life?

Over a period of three years, Jesus taught His disciples how to live without being overcome by fear and worry. On one occasion, He told them:

> Consider the lilies of the field, how they grow; they toil not, neither do they spin: And yet I say unto you, That

even Solomon in all his glory was not arrayed like one of these. Wherefore, if God so clothe the grass of the field, which today is, and to morrow is cast into the oven, shall he not much more clothe you, O ye of little faith? (Matthew 6:28-30)

Jesus said all this after having just said:

Take no thought for your life, what ye shall eat, or what ye shall drink; nor yet for your body, what ye shall put on. Is not the life more than meat, and the body than raiment. . . . Which of you by taking thought can add one cubit unto his stature? (Matthew 6:25, 27)

Now let me explain what I believe Jesus meant and did not mean by these passages. First of all, in saying what He did about taking no thought for our lives, I do not think Jesus was advocating for personal neglect or for unpreparedness. On a personal note, Deborah and I have always been advocates for preparedness. Let me give an example. Back in 1999, we helped organize the Y2K task force in our hometown. During that year, we helped many families in our community learn how to be prepared for disaster (not just Y2K). Then, when nothing significant happened on New Year's Day, some mocked what we had done. I heard one well-known Christian leader say, *after the fact,* on his radio program that he had known all along that nothing was going to happen and that those who had prepared were a bunch of idiots. As I listened to him speak, I wondered why during the year prior, when technology experts and those considered computer savvy were giving out warnings about computer crashes, that this leader with a public forum had not raised a voice to counter the efforts at preparedness. Be it as it may, our involvement with Y2K was not really about a catastrophe happening on a specific calendar date, but for us it was a wake-up call in realizing that our society has become so dependent on the local supermarket and our power grid that most would have scarcely enough food, water, and fuel to last only a few days even in a small-scale crisis. A case in point happened in a town I was in when some teenagers were seen playing around the city-water site. The authorities then became concerned that the water could have been tampered with and instructed the townspeople not to drink, cook, or bathe in that water until it was tested. Needless to say, the bottled water in the grocery stores disappeared from the shelves by that afternoon. This was not even a big scare, and the water proved to be safe after all.

Jesus' words about the lilies of the field were a much-needed exhortation to trust God in all aspects of our lives. At the same time, however, Jesus was talking to an agrarian people who knew and practiced preparedness as they utilized their skills in growing and properly storing food for the winter. If this were not true, Solomon would not have praised the ordinary ant in saying:

> [C]onsider her ways, and be wise: Which having no guide, overseer, or ruler, Providenth her meat in the summer, and gathereth her food in the harvest. (Proverbs 6:6-8)

Personally, I think it is an embarrassment to our federal government that they would go so far as to vilify people who harvest and store their food for the winter as "hoarders" when this has been common practice in the world practically from the beginning of man until now.

If you have followed our ministry for any length of time, then you know that we have rarely talked about preparedness. Yet in bygone days, it used to be a very normal task for people to cut firewood, tend the livestock, and plant or harvest the fields; so while it is not my intention to get into a lengthy discussion on the practical matters of life, let me say in passing that it would not hurt to consider the situations in which we live. While many of us may be locked into conditions or locations that make change nearly impossible, it doesn't hurt, if you have the opportunity, to consider what would be best for you and your family in the future. Especially if you live in a highly populated city, it does not take much imagination to think of the crime and looting that could ensue after a serious power failure or disaster.

In the Shadow of His Wings

Now, having said all this, let's return to the words of Jesus when He said that we should take no thought for our lives. The fact is, we are only as safe as the Lord enables us to be. Hence, regardless of our situation in life, our only real option for safety is to place our lives and our futures in the hands of the Lord. In our home, we love Psalm 57:1:

> Be merciful unto me, O God, be merciful unto me: for my soul trusteth in thee: yea, in the shadow of thy wings will I make my refuge, until these calamities be overpast.

While it would be wise to make whatever practical measures we can for the future, none of us are immune from disaster, loss, disease, or theft. To be truly prepared to face the future means above all to be spiritually prepared—and that means having a right relationship with the Lord.

Now is the time for Christians to "lay aside every weight, and the sin which doth so easily beset us, and let us run with patience the race that is set before us" (Hebrews 12:1). In other words, like the athlete set out to run a race, we need to strip off any excess baggage that would hinder us from giving the Lord our very best. God's overwhelming desire for us is that we walk with Him with all our heart, mind, soul, and strength (Mark 12:30).

I would like to finish this chapter with some thoughts about what it means to walk in God's peace.

First of all, let me say that just as the Gospel is the power of God unto salvation to everyone who believes (Romans 1:16), it is also the avenue to peace with God:

> Therefore being justified by faith, we have peace with God through our Lord Jesus Christ. (Romans 5:1)

> **Modern-day church leadership has left today's Christian with a sense of insufficiency of the Gospel and has instead presented an array of substitutes.**

All of us who have entered into union with God through believing the Gospel—namely that Jesus purchased our salvation fully through His death on the Cross—have God's peace available to us. Today, it seems that many proclaiming Christians do not really have a sense of God's peace (which I believe is why so many are turning to mystical practices). I am fully persuaded it is because they have become removed from the simplicity of the Gospel. The modern-day church leadership has left today's Christian with a sense of insufficiency of the Gospel and has instead presented an array of substitutes to include such things as relaxation exercises, breath prayers, Lectio Divina, Yoga, and contemplative prayer all with an empty promise of delivering peace and God's presence when in fact the Gospel is all sufficient for that purpose. Through the Gospel, Jesus opened the door of salvation, promising to live (abide) in us:

> To whom God would make known what is the riches of the glory of this mystery among the Gentiles; which is Christ in you. (Colossians 1:27)

And:

> [H]ereby we know that he abideth in us, by the Spirit which he hath given u. (1 John 3:24)

As we live by faith, we will enjoy the benefits of God's peace. And as I mentioned earlier, when Jesus pointed out that we should take no thought for our lives, He indicated that our lives should be free of fear and worry. God wants us to strive for this goal and attain it as well. Jesus then ended His statements with the clause, "O ye of little faith" (Matthew 6:30). Simply put, our freedom from fear and worry are only available to us as we allow our faith and trust in the Lord to grow. A perfect example of this is where Jesus, while walking on the water, welcomed Peter to come out and meet Him. Peter, whose life was a mixture of self-confidence and faith, was OK as long as he kept his eyes on Jesus, but as he turned his eyes to the wind and the waves, that confidence soon left him. It was the same self-confidence that led him to tell Jesus that he would never deny Him only to be dashed later, causing him to weep bitterly. But it was a good thing for Peter that his self-confidence was so utterly dashed because he was later able to become a great hero of the faith as he found he had abundant and sufficient grace through Christ (even to the point where he was able to go to his death for the sake of Christ) as he put his confidence in Jesus alone. In this one illustration of meeting Jesus on the water, we find the secret of faith that enabled Peter to walk in an abiding peace. Isaiah was inspired by this same kind of faith when he penned the words:

> Thou wilt keep him in perfect peace, whose mind is stayed on thee: because he trusteth in thee. Trust ye in the LORD for ever: for in the LORD JEHOVAH is everlasting strength. (Isaiah 26:3-4)

If we can make ready for the future in practical ways, it would be good to do so. But, above all, we must not neglect spiritual preparedness. We will all need spiritual strength (that only God can give) to face the future. That means drawing strength from God by reading and pondering on His Word. Then, it means applying that Word to our lives. My prayer is that the words of Scripture, like that from Isaiah 26 above, will be a reality for you and me; but this can only happen as we forsake the phony, unreliable comforts of this life and trust the Lord to be our strength. Yes, walking through this life can be heartbreaking and terrifying at times, but as we keep our mind stayed on Him, trusting Him, we can walk forward in His peace.

The Bible says that those who trust the Lord shall not be disappointed (Psalm 34:22). As we watch the world falling apart, there really is no other option than to trust the Lord; thus, may our resolve be to trust Him as fully as we can, even though things will not always go the way we want or hope for; but we can be comforted and assured in knowing that for those who "love God" and are "called according to his purpose," "all things work together for good" (Romans 8:28). God has His best intentions in mind for us, and He will not be prevented from accomplishing it. One thing that can give us a sense of stability and peace of mind is knowing that even though God allows evil to happen in the world, when we are "sealed" in Christ, He will never leave us nor forsake us.

> Therefore being justified by faith, we have peace with God through our Lord Jesus Christ: By whom also we have access by faith into this grace wherein we stand, and rejoice in hope of the glory of God. (Romans 5: 1-2)

Chapter 13

How Much Does the Gospel Weigh?

The Gospel is a standard and the central theme of the entire Bible. We can think of it like a balancing scale, weighing truth against error. But how much does the Gospel weigh? That might sound like a foolish question, but let's take a moment to see how a balancing scale works. Basically, it is an arm extending from both sides with a fulcrum in the middle. A standardized weight is then placed on one side, and subsequently everything placed on the other arm of the scale will be measured and valued by that standardized weight. A false scale, as Proverbs states, uses a deceptive weight purported to be a standardized weight when it really is not. Consequently, everything weighed on that scale for the next five, ten, or a thousand years will have an erroneous result. A false scale just keeps on lying because the standard is wrong.

If we are going to use the Gospel as a standardized weight, knowing how much the Gospel weighs might be worth pondering. The prophet Zechariah gives us a clue:

> And I said unto them, If ye think good, give me my price; and if not, forbear. So they weighed for my price thirty pieces of silver. And the LORD said unto me, Cast it unto the potter: a goodly price that I was prised at of them. And

> I took the thirty pieces of silver, and cast them to the potter in the house of the LORD. (Zechariah 11:12-13)

Again, what was forecast in the Old Testament is fulfilled in the New, and in Matthew 26:15, we see that when Judas asked the chief priests what price they would give for delivering Jesus to them, it says, "they covenanted with him for thirty pieces of silver." This was the value the priests of that day placed on Jesus. But what follows is most significant. When Judas returns later to the chief priests and elders, he says:

> I have sinned in that I have betrayed the innocent blood. And they said, What is that to us? see thou to that. And he cast down the pieces of silver in the temple, and departed, and went and hanged himself. And the chief priests took the silver pieces, and said, It is not lawful for to put them into the treasury, because it is the price of blood. And they took counsel, and bought with them the potter's field, to bury strangers in. (Matthew 27:4-7)

It was the chief priests of that day, not Judas, who placed the value of Jesus and measured out thirty pieces of silver.

> Then was fulfilled that which was spoken by Jeremy the prophet, saying, And they took the thirty pieces of silver, the price of him that was valued, whom they of the children of Israel did value. (Matthew 27:9)

But when Judas threw the money down on the temple floor, he realized the money was worthless in comparison with the man he had betrayed. Even more so, it was a prophetic statement of God from centuries past that the value placed on Jesus would be as erroneous as it could possibly be.

An Immeasurable Price

The price of Jesus and what He did for us, weighed out, is immeasurable. When weighed against anything else, the Gospel always tips the scale. It is the standardized weight that no matter what you compare it with, the item you are weighing will come up lacking.

Over the centuries, man has come up with all sorts of ideas and philosophies that have only served to prove how priceless the Gospel really is. Jesus truly is the Son of God, and He truly paid our debt on the Cross. But today, more than ever, the Gospel is under attack, and we need to faithfully hold on to it and defend it as the standard that is true.

> Over the centuries, man has come up with all sorts of ideas and philosophies that have only served to prove how priceless the Gospel really is.

We are all too familiar with all the vain teachings that have been used to discredit the Gospel message over the last two thousand years. Paul warns to steer away from such teachings:

> Beware lest any man spoil you through philosophy and vain deceit, after the tradition of men, after the rudiments of the world, and not after Christ. (Colossians 2:8)

To Timothy, whom he regarded as a son in the faith, Paul has a strong exhortation at the end of his first epistle:

> O Timothy, keep that which is committed to thy trust, avoiding profane and vain babblings, and oppositions of science falsely so called. (1 Timothy 6:20)

Having strongly opposed the Gospel in the past, Paul knew what it is to be greatly deceived by one's own reasonings and the thoughts of the culture. He was recognized as one of the greatest intellectuals of his time, yet one day on a road to Damascus, he discovered that all his profound learning did not measure up to God's standard. Paul later used his intellectual abilities to become one of the strongest defenders of the faith in human history.

Today, there is a whole barrage of religious leaders who use their intellectual prowess to persuade Christians to abandon the fundamentals of the Christian faith for something more intellectually palatable to the postmodern "progressive" mind. These leaders are holding up a new standard suggesting the standard of the Gospel is outdated and a new standardized weight needs to be placed on the balance. Many of these emerging progressive leaders make it sound like they have made a new discovery that no one has thought of before they came along. Using their philosophical reasonings, you will hear them question how a God of love could send His Son to die a cruel death on a cross for the sins of others. They will further maintain that a God of love would never send anyone to Hell—a place that in their own minds does not exist. Human reason then, and not the teachings of the Bible, becomes the test of truth. The long-held truths of the Bible must now bend to intellectual fabrications of what God must be like. Yes, a new standard has replaced the standard of the Gospel by which truth and all Christian doctrine can be weighed. But this is nothing new, as philosophers of the past have believed that the human intellect is a wellspring of innate knowledge and ultimately the only source and deciding factor of truth.

"Science Falsely So Called"

Some arrive at many of the same conclusions from a slightly different vantage point. They hold that the realm of science (a "new" quantum science they say) offers the wealth of knowledge we are looking for. Some have suggested that if we look at the physical world at the sub-atomic level, we will actually find God. At first, it seems like a wonderful idea to think that we can prove to an unbelieving world the existence of God. A good idea, that is, until we realize we are again talking about another Gospel—for to "discover" that God exists in all creation at the sub-atomic level suggests a panentheistic view of God. Yet Romans 1 distinguishes the creature from Creator (verse 25). In fact, the panentheistic view contradicts and discredits the whole Genesis account. Paul clarifies there are two realities—physical and spiritual—and they are not the same (1 Corinthians 15:35-50). From Genesis to Revelation, the Bible actually makes it very clear that God is separate from His creation. My question is, if God is spiritual rather than physical, when the scientists discover God at the sub-atomic level, what god will that actually be?

Needless to say, what is being passed off as cutting-edge spirituality is what Paul warned about when he talked about "vain philosophies" and "science falsely so called." The fact is, God has given mankind the ability to reason and to make empirical observations, but no amount of human reasoning and scientific experimentation, in and of themselves, will enable man to arrive at God outside of that which is revealed in the Bible.

For the Christian, the Gospel has been and always will be that standardized weight and the pivot from which we measure truth from error. Today, more than ever, the church is plagued by such a vast assortment of spiritualities and false teachings, some of which are so subtle, that even the most discerning are vulnerable to dangerous deception.

The sad truth is that most church-going, self-proclaiming Christians today do not understand the times in which we live and would prefer that "negative" "trouble-making" organizations such as Lighthouse Trails would cease to exist. But as long as the Lord upholds it, and in spite of many adversaries, those of us who defend the faith and contend for His Word are often reminded of our Lord's words of admonition to work "while it is day: the night cometh, when no man can work" (John 9:4).

However, something needs to be said here: Although Lighthouse Trails exists as a source of information, this is not our highest calling. We believe God has called us to work "[f]or the perfecting of the saints, for the work of the ministry, for the edifying of the body of Christ" (Ephesians 4:12). For the "perfecting of the saints" to happen, Christians need to learn to think on their own. Too many ministries exist that create a following of dependents rather than discipling men and women of God who are strong in the faith. The Lord is our strength and in Him and His Word we have everything we need to live an overcoming life (2 Peter 1:3). Paul put it succinctly when he said this concerning our Lord:

> In whom are hid all the treasures of wisdom and knowledge.
> And this I say, lest any man should beguile you with enticing words. (Colossians 2:3-4)

Let us cling to the priceless treasure we have in Christ. None of us will ever have a perfect hold of all Christian doctrine—as Paul says we see as looking through a glass darkly (1 Corinthians 13:12), but if we hold fast to our Savior and Lord, hide His Word in our hearts, and let His Spirit teach us (1 Corinthians 2:13), we will have all we need to get us through.

How much does the Gospel weigh? More than the weight of all the sins of mankind put together. Christ's death on the Cross bore that load, and nothing can take its place.

Chapter 14

Neglecting to Test the Spirits—A Tragedy of Enormous Proportions*

From the onset of Lighthouse Trails in 2002, we have endeavored to be connected with the body of believers scattered throughout the world who are very concerned, as we are, with the state of the church today. Many of our readers have told us they feel very alone and even ostracized in witnessing today's apostasy. We know firsthand how it feels to be labeled troublemakers for having legitimate concerns about what is happening in many churches.

We too have felt disillusioned as we have watched a gradual departure take place from the Word of God. Pulpits throughout the land, many of which formerly proclaimed the biblical Gospel of God's saving grace through the sacrifice on the Cross, now espouse an assortment of ecumenism, progressivism, New Age, mysticism, wokeism, and a social-justice gospel. It is no wonder that God, in referring to the lukewarm church, warns that He is ready to "spew thee" out of His mouth (Revelation 3:16). How much better it would have been if churches and their pastors had stuck with John 3:16!

Many discerning believers now find they have become watchmen on the wall, compelled by God to sound out a clear warning of

---

*This chapter is co-authored with the editors at Lighthouse Trails Publishing.

great seduction in the church. In fact, it appears that God has been calling out believers from various denominations to stand up and be counted among those who refuse to comply with the compromised experience-driven Christianity of today.

On a daily basis now, we witness our very Earth in what seems like birth pangs—be it nuclear threat, extreme weather conditions, earthquakes, diseases, terrorism, unspeakable violence, wars and rumors of war, and basically the destruction of society's moral grounding taking as victims countless numbers of children and youth. Sadly, most people seem oblivious to what is happening (or may see something is amiss but do not turn to the Lord and His prophetic Word for understanding and guidance). But make no mistake, God is sounding out a warning to fulfill that which He has said He will do.

Even now, while the reality of the Antichrist and a one-world government and unified religion is looming closer all the time, preachers and teachers are sitting at their desks inking out sermons that discredit Bible prophecy.

A Creeping Effect

The changes have been gradual but steady and relentless. Everywhere we turn, embellishments are being added to Christianity as if to improve it. The old ways do not seem to satisfy anymore. A great influx of new teachings and practices have exchanged the God who is depicted in the pages of the Bible with a deity much more palatable to the postmodern (or what some are now calling *metamodern*) so-called progressive mind.

Brennan Manning, the Catholic contemplative mystic, illustrates this when he states in one of his books "the god who exacts the last drop of blood from His Son, so that His just anger, evoked by sin, may be appeased is not the God revealed by and in Jesus Christ. And if he is not the God of Jesus, he does not exist."[1] This is really a denial of the penal substitutionary atonement of Jesus Christ. It's an attitude that is far more common than most realize. Let us step back for a moment to see how this paradigm shift has developed. Such a statement did not come out of the blue, but as Ray Yungen suggests, a "creeping" effect made it all possible.[2]

Over the years, Christian leaders and pastors have stopped defending the faith and have exchanged the Word of God for things that outwardly appear very spiritual, promising a "quantum leap" into a "new spirituality." Though we have always witnessed those who deny Christ's substitutionary death on the Cross, most of this kind of thought and teaching has been kept out of the evangelical/Protestant church. But as the walls of biblical truth were gradually torn down, it is no longer unusual to hear this kind of teaching in Christian colleges and seminaries or in books published by Christian publishers. Much of what we see today began with men who pioneered the way to apostasy, then, like a domino effect, these ideas caught on and accelerated to the unbiblical thoughts and teachings we are seeing in so many Christian circles today.

> A great influx of new teachings and practices have exchanged the God of the Bible with a deity much more palatable to the postmodern so-called "progressive" mind.

You may be saying to yourself right now—"I've never heard a pastor or Christian leader deny the atonement." Let's remember that Satan is the father of deception, and it is his goal to make deception look very much like the real thing. For example, a term often used in describing Jesus in many Christian circles today is "servant leader." Sounds innocent enough, right? But when Jesus is referred to as the perfect servant leader, it is another way of saying that Jesus was the perfect role model or example of someone who knew how to lay down

His life for others. This is true, of course—He continually laid down His life for others; however, today's "new spirituality" church takes it a step further by saying it is wrong to say that Jesus' death on the Cross was actually a substitute for sin—yes, he was an example of being a servant as seen in His going to the Cross, but that is all. That is what Brennan Manning was referring to when he said that God would not require blood from His son to pay for the sins of others.

What is interesting about Manning's quote on the previous page, taken from his 2003 book *Above All*, is that it is nearly a word-for-word rendering of several lines from New Age sympathizer and mystic William Shannon's 1995 book *Silence on Fire*.[3] This book is the biography of Thomas Merton who possibly had more to do than anyone else in giving mysticism (namely contemplative prayer) that initial push whereby it has now avalanched into the mainline evangelical/Protestant churches. But it all began as a creeping or rippling effect with the initial momentum almost imperceptibly slow.

Over the last few decades, countless pastors and religious leaders across North America have grabbed for their evening reading books written by mystics like Henri Nouwen, hoping to glean something to carry them to the next level of spirituality. Unfortunately, that *quantum* leap ends in the web of apostasy. As you may know, Henri Nouwen (also a great admirer of Thomas Merton) wrote in a provocative intellectual style that has intrigued many pastors, but what happens when these pastors stumble upon these words:

> Today I personally believe that while Jesus came to open the door to God's house, all human beings can walk through that door, whether they know about Jesus or not. Today I see it as my call to help every person claim *his or her own way to God*.[4] (emphasis added)

Henri Nouwen said these words toward the end of his life after spending years involved with mysticism. And yet, pastors, leaders, and professors are enamored with Nouwen. And on goes that seemingly subtle creeping in of deception, slowly but surely.

Testing the Spirits

If there is one thing we don't hear much about from today's Christian leaders and pastors, it is the importance of testing the spirits. The idea comes from the Bible in 1 John 4:1, which states:

> Beloved, believe not every spirit, but try [test] the spirits whether they are of God: because many false prophets are gone out into the world.

This can relate both to the experiential and the doctrinal. With either, we need to remember that not every experience and not every doctrine is "of God" because indeed there are "many false prophets" in the world and in the church today, and there are many voices that are not from God.

"The Voice of Love"—Is There a Need to Test the Spirits?

The question of whether or not we need to test the spirits gets various answers depending on whom you are talking to and listening to. According to the Catholic mystic Basil Pennington in his classic book *Centering Prayer* (who, along with Thomas Keating and Thomas Merton, introduced "centering prayer" to the layperson), there is no need to test the spirits when in the state of "silence" induced by practicing contemplative meditation or centering prayer. Pennington stated:

> Isn't there a danger, if we leave off thinking and judging and just be quiet, that we might be opening not to God and his activity but to the activity of the evil spirits? St. John of the Cross brings out in his teaching that when we

enter into contemplative prayer, we need have no fear of the deceptions of the Evil One, because he cannot touch us at that level of our being. . . . He cannot himself penetrate into our spiritual being. There is danger, a need for discernment, in active prayer, in which we are using our imagination and feelings, for he can influence these. But in Centering Prayer we ignore these faculties and simply let images and feelings float away. They do not affect our prayer, so the Evil One cannot touch it. We are engaged at a level that the Lord has made his own through grace and baptism. We are out of the Devil's reach. Only God can penetrate this level of our being. So we are completely safe in contemplative prayer.[5]

So, in other words, according to Pennington, the enemy can get to us in regular prayer where our minds are actively engaged, but when we enter into the contemplative "sacred space" (i.e., stopping all thought and putting our minds into neutral by repeating a word or phrase or focusing on the breath), we have no danger of being influenced or touched by Satan. What Pennington is proposing is very scary because according to contemplative spirituality leaders (of which there are many today), the objective is to hear God's voice (Thomas Keating says, "God's first language is silence,"[6] and Brennan Manning calls it "the Voice of Love"[7]). If we go by Pennington's advice, we do not need to question this voice of love we hear during contemplative meditation (i.e., it will *always* be good and *always* from God).

Sarah Young's "Jesus"—The Voice of God?

We know that Sarah Young, the late author of *Jesus Calling*, was an advocate of contemplative prayer; so did she believe that these "messages" from "Jesus" in *Jesus Calling* do not need to be tested and are absolutely, without a doubt, from God (as

Pennington believes)? Young never says that they *do* need to be tested. And from what we have observed for several years from church leaders and pastors, they don't believe her messages from "Jesus" need to be tested either. A list of endorsers compiled by the publisher of her book includes the names of many mainstream evangelical/Christian figures such as: David Jeremiah, Lysa Terkeurst, Max Lucado, Kay Warren, Bart Millard, Lee Strobel, Craig Groeschel, Henry Cloud, Jack Graham, and numerous others.[8] Do you recall any of these leaders saying to test the spirit that is in *Jesus Calling*? *We* can't recall such a thing.

Warren B. Smith discusses testing the spirits in his book, *"Another Jesus" Calling*:

> There is no evidence that the spirits are being tested to see if Sarah Young's best-selling messages are from the true Jesus Christ.
>
> Given that Sarah Young's "Jesus" is delivering messages that are being read around the world, it is imperative for readers to know if she is really hearing from the true Jesus Christ.
>
> Scripture's warning to believers to "try the spirits" (1 John 4:1) is nowhere to be found in *Jesus Calling*. To the contrary, when Sarah Young's "Jesus" is quoted in *Jesus Calling* as saying, "You must learn to discern what is My voice and what is not,"[9] he gives her some very dangerous counsel. With no mention of 1 Timothy 4:1's warning about "seducing spirits," he says, "Ask My Spirit to give you this discernment."[10] But if the "Jesus" that Sarah Young is listening to is not the true Jesus Christ, then this false "Christ" is instructing her to ask *his* spirit to tell her what is true and what is not. Consequently, instead of *testing* the spirit, she is asking and *trusting* the spirit that she should be testing. This can only lead to greater deception and confusion. This counsel by Sarah Young's "Jesus" cleverly works to prevent

the detection of a counterfeit "Jesus," which obviously plays right into the hands of our spiritual Adversary.[11]

What Is the Test?

Sometimes we are asked, what is the criterion for deciding whether or not a doctrine or practice is biblical or validates criticism? There is one test that we have used consistently from the inception of Lighthouse Trails. The Book of Proverbs says:

> A false balance is abomination to the Lord: but a just weight is his delight. (Proverbs 11:1)

And again from Proverbs:

> Divers weights are an abomination unto the LORD; and a false balance is not good. (Proverbs 20:23)

It is interesting that Solomon, considered the wisest man who ever lived, placed such emphasis on accurate scales. It is even more amazing that God would call false scales an abomination—amazing only until we realize that God is speaking of the spiritual—not just physical scales here.

So what we are looking for is a spiritual balancing scale—something that will reappear throughout the Bible—through the Old and New Testaments. There *is* such a scale, a consistent theme, which John refers to in his first epistle:

> Beloved, believe not every spirit, but try the spirits whether they are of God: because many false prophets are gone out into the world. Hereby know ye the Spirit of God: Every spirit that confesseth that Jesus Christ is come in the flesh is of God: And every spirit that confesseth not that Jesus Christ is come in the flesh is not of God: and this is that spirit of antichrist, whereof ye have heard that

it should come; and even now already is it in the world. (1 John 4:1-3)

Some Bible commentators have believed that John was referring here to a particular sect who denied that Jesus Christ actually came in a human body. If that is all John meant, then this passage is of little relevance to us today because you will scarcely find anyone who does not believe that Jesus as a historical figure was a man who walked the Earth. But the name Jesus Christ in this passage is not a historical term; it is a name loaded with meaning—referring to Jesus as the Messiah, God come in the flesh, our Savior and Redeemer who atoned for our sins. If we look at the context of 1 John 4, we can verify that this is what John is talking about because in it he says:

> And we have seen and do testify that the Father sent the Son to be the Saviour of the world. (1 John 4:14)

What John is saying here is, *I am referring to the Jesus I wrote about in my gospel—the Word made flesh who in the beginning was with God and was God* (see John chapter 1).

This is the balancing scale we have been looking for. Just as all human history and our blessed hope hinges on what Jesus did on the Cross, so too we can weigh a doctrine or practice by whether or not it agrees with the fact that we are justified by faith alone through the atoning, redemptive work of Christ on the Cross. The question then is, does a particular doctrine or teaching agree with the Gospel the apostles all preached?

With this discerning tool in hand, if you stop to measure all the world's religions and systems, you will find that all these are opposed to the Gospel. The natural man will not acknowledge the need for a Savior; consequently the *world's* belief systems (except biblical Christianity) are works based—believing it is possible to earn our way into Heaven (or some version of eternal life) or to become "Christ-like" through mysticism and "spiritual disciplines" which is the foundation and thrust of Spiritual Formation/contemplative prayer. But the Gospel says it is not possible. John knew all too well the contrariness of the natural man and the world's belief systems. That is why in the same chapter of his epistle, he offers another test:

> [H]e that knoweth God heareth us; he that is not of God heareth not us. Hereby know we the spirit of truth, and the spirit of error. (1 John 4:6)

In other words, John is saying that when the world rejects you for sharing the Gospel, it is because the Spirit of truth is not in them.

Whichever way you look at it, the Gospel is the fulcrum of our balance in discerning truth from error. When Lighthouse Trails Publishing began, this became, and has always been, our standard of truth, and we are compelled to speak up—because as believers in Christ, we are called to defend the Gospel.

The Gospel is the most precious thing on God's heart, and it is worthy of our defense and protection. Wouldn't we, as Christian believers, like to be remembered as men or women after God's own heart (1 Samuel 13: 14)? If so, then let's defend the Gospel.

A Moment of Truth With a Moment of Terror

In a discussion about testing the spirits, it's definitely worth discussing contemplative pioneer Richard Foster. After all, the objective that drives the contemplative prayer movement is to "hear" the voice of God. Foster had something very interesting to say about demons and contemplative prayer. In a roundabout way, it was a moment of truth for him because we have only heard him say it once. And it seems like a contradiction to Pennington's advice even though Foster got it wrong, too, as Roger Oakland explains in his book, *Faith Undone*:

> Proponents of contemplative prayer say the purpose of contemplative prayer is to tune in with God and hear His

Neglecting to Test the Spirits

voice. However, Richard Foster claims that practitioners must use caution. He admits that in contemplative prayer "we are entering deeply into the spiritual realm"[12] and that sometimes it is not the realm of God even though it is "supernatural."[13] He admits there are spiritual beings and that a prayer of protection should be said beforehand something to the effect of "All dark and evil spirits must now leave."[14] Where in Scripture do we find such a prayer? Where in witchcraft?

I wonder if all these Christians who now practice contemplative prayer are following Foster's advice. Whether they are or not, they have put themselves in spiritual harm's way. Nowhere in Scripture are we required to pray a prayer of protection before we pray. The fact that Foster recognizes contemplative prayer is dangerous and opens the door to the fallen spirit world is very revealing. What is this—praying to the God of the Bible but instead reaching demons? Maybe contemplative prayer should be renamed contemplative terror.

While Foster has repeatedly said that contemplative prayer is for everyone, he contradicts himself when he says it is only for a select group and not for the "novice."[15] He says not everyone is ready and equipped to listen to God's voice through the "all embracing silence."[16]

This is amazing. Foster admits that contemplative prayer is dangerous and will possibly take the participant into demonic realms, but he gives a disclaimer saying not everyone is ready for it. My question is, who is ready, and how will they know they are ready? What about all the young people in the emergent church (aka progressive) movement? Are they ready? Or are they going into demonic altered states of consciousness completely unaware? Given Foster's admission of the danger, he does great damage when he contradicts himself and says, "We should all, without shame, enroll in the school of contemplative prayer."[17]

Foster's implication that *some* contemplative prayer is safe is terribly mistaken. *No* contemplative prayer is biblical or safe—even the most mature of the Christian mystical leaders proved susceptible to its demonic pull. Thomas Merton, at the end of his life, said he wanted to be the best Buddhist he could be. Henri Nouwen, at the end of *his* life, said all paths lead to God. This was the spiritual "fruit" of their lives after years of practicing mystical prayer.

[In relation to mysticism and contemplative prayer], the real question is whether or not the realm of the silence is God's realm or Satan's (i.e., light or darkness). The Bible tells us that Satan is very deceptive, and what can often look good is not good at all:

"And no marvel; for Satan himself is transformed into an angel of light. Therefore it is no great thing if his ministers also be transformed as the ministers of righteousness" (2 Corinthians 11:14-15).[18]

Regarding Foster's "prayer of protection," Mike Oppenheimer states:

Asking God to protect us as we enter into a place He does not ever tell us to go is testing God. Not a good position to put oneself in considering the ramifications.[19]

Oppenheimer makes a good point. And sad to say, given the fact that much of today's Christianity has become immersed in that place Richard Foster calls them to; in essence, the church is testing God (which we are not to do) but *not* testing the spirits (as the Bible instructs us to do). Again, scary—as well as tragic.

Living Inside a Bubble

If only pastors and church leaders realized the great responsibility they have in helping to watch over and protect the sheep. When we first began Lighthouse Trails Publishing, we contacted our pastor at that time, trying to encourage him to warn his congregation of the apostasy that was beginning to creep into the church back then. His reply was that he lives inside a bubble and consequently sees no need to warn his congregation about anything as long as he keeps expounding the Word to them. Our reply to him was "*you* may be living in a bubble, but your congregation does not." The question is this: if it is not the pastor's job to warn his congregation of impending spiritual danger, whose job is it? In the Old Testament, the prophets referred to individuals with this kind of responsibility as watchmen or shepherds. The prophet Zechariah, for example, has much to say about the responsibilities of a shepherd in chapters 10 and 11. In referring to the spiritual condition of his day, he said:

> For the idols have spoken vanity, and the diviners have seen a lie, and have told false dreams; they comfort in vain: therefore they went their way as a flock, they were troubled, because there was no shepherd. (Zechariah 10:2)

Nothing could speak more succinctly of the condition of the church today. We never dreamed in all our years as Christians there would ever be such blatant heresy as we see in the organized Christian church today. Yet this is exactly what is happening. We should be mourning as God surely must be mourning.

If a pastor feels it is not his calling to warn his congregation, remember that the closest New Testament equivalent to the Old Testament watchmen or shepherds is the position of a pastor. There is a time for speaking uplifting encouraging words of peace and comfort—but when ravenous wolves are about, is it not wiser to "reprove, rebuke, exhort with all longsuffering and doctrine" (2 Timothy 4:2)?

The Cost

The North American church is on borrowed time. We have become weak and spoiled, and it is time to change course and return to a no-compromise faith—the kind many of us had when we first became Christians. To straddle the fence and to exhibit no discernment, as has been the case for far too long, has cost the church dearly and could mean a steady erosion of biblical faith and a fall into the mire of full-blown apostasy.

While there are many forces at work attempting to strip the identity of Jesus of who He is and what He came for, we should never forget that in Him we have a priceless treasure. Isaiah said of Him, "his name shall be called Wonderful, Counsellor, The mighty God, The everlasting Father, The Prince of Peace" (Isaiah 9:6). Most importantly, Jesus came to redeem us from our sins:

> In whom we have redemption through his blood, the forgiveness of sins, according to the riches of his grace. (Ephesians 1:7)

When Jesus spoke of the kingdom of Heaven, he used a number of illustrations, one of which should have special significance in our churches today:

> Again, the kingdom of heaven is like unto treasure hid in a field; the which when a man hath found, he hideth, and for joy thereof goeth and selleth all that he hath, and buyeth that field. (Matthew 13:44)

While the "progressive" (i.e., postmodern*) Christians of today are casting accurate biblical doctrine on the dung heap more than ever, we should be holding on to it as something truly sacred, for it is biblical doctrine that defines our faith and gives to us living water. Hebrews 4:12 tells us:

> For the word of God is quick, and powerful, and sharper than any twoedged sword, piercing even to the dividing asunder of soul and spirit, and of the joints and marrow, and is a discerner of the thoughts and intents of the heart.

No wonder the devil wants to undermine and get rid of the Word of God; and he is attempting to do it through many who *call* themselves Christians.

Contending for the faith may cost us everything we have, but it is worth it—a jewel far above any price. This life will soon be over, but eternity will last a very long time. Shouldn't we be putting our treasures in Heaven no matter what it may cost us now?

> **Contending for the faith may cost us everything we have, but it is worth it—a jewel far above any price.**

> Again, the kingdom of heaven is like unto a merchant man, seeking goodly pearls: Who, when he had found one pearl of great price, went and sold all that he had, and bought it. (Matthew 13:45-46)

---

*Keep an eye out for a relatively new term—"metamodern spirituality"—which is being used to describe those who have moved *beyond* and *ahead* of the postmodern /emergent movement.

Now Is the Time

In the Old Testament, the Israelites took great pains in transporting the Ark of the Covenant. According to the instructions given by God to Moses (Exodus 25:13-15), the Ark was to be carried by staves (poles) on the shoulders of the children of the Levites (1 Chronicles 15:15). However, in 1 Chronicles 13:7-10, contrary to Moses' specific instructions, they put the Ark on a cart to be pulled by oxen. But the unexpected happened. When "Uzza put forth his hand to hold the ark; for the oxen stumbled . . . the anger of the LORD was kindled against Uzza, and he smote him" (1 Chronicles 13:9-10). The Levites, who were the "pastors" of that day, were careless about following Moses' instructions; and it ended up costing a life. The Ark of the Covenant was a type and foreshadowing of the Gospel. It was sprinkled with blood to symbolize Christ's death on the Cross. Today, similar to back then, so many pastors and Christian leaders have become careless about the Gospel. And it has become so evident that the church has been duped into thinking all is well and there is no need to test the spirits and practice discernment. The result of such neglect is truly a tragedy of enormous proportions.

If we love Jesus Christ and His Word, and if we really want to serve Him, now is the time to, by faith, place our lives under the care and guidance of the true Shepherd, leaning on the Scriptures as we exercise discernment. Whatever the cost. We are invited to the wedding feast, ready to meet our Savior, with wicks trimmed and lamps burning. Now is the time to make ready.

Chapter 15

Guard Your Heart With All Diligence

The "Covid years" were an educational experience regarding the nature of people's hearts. I believe it would be accurate to say we have entered perilous times; and where it will take us in the future, we don't know except that we must always keep our hope in the Lord, even as we see Bible prophecy being fulfilled. Meanwhile, guarding (keeping) our hearts is perhaps more vital now than it has ever been before in our lives as we witness all that is happening in the world. Jesus warned:

> And many false prophets shall rise, and shall deceive many. And because iniquity shall abound, the love of many shall wax cold. (Matthew 24:11-12)

If we look at the context of this Scripture, we will see that Jesus is talking about what will precede the end of the world; but it's easy to see that things are already astir, and just as we see in our weather how one season changes to the next, we can see the clouds of change approaching.

Guarding Our Hearts When Fear Rules

During the Covid period of time, scientific studies contradicted what the media was telling us to do, so it was quite difficult, if not impossible, to know what the best course of action was in any given situation. But my point here is not really about who was right and who was wrong as much as how people's hearts were responding—some showing civility and others hardness of heart. I understood in a whole new way how a wicked person like Adolf Hitler was able to dupe an entire country through propaganda and fear mongering.

Machiavelli pointed out in his book, *The Prince*, you can rule an entire country through fear and compliance, where morality is superseded by craft and deceit in governing the affairs of men. This is the man who came up with the well-known and unfortunately much-used maxim, "The ends justify the means." We see this operating today.

In the final chapter of this book, let us remind ourselves that God has given us the incentive to guard our hearts through verses utilizing the word "keep," such as the following:

> Keep [guard] thy heart with all diligence; for out of it are the issues of life. (Proverbs 4:23)

> Lay hands suddenly on no man, neither be partaker of other men's sins: *keep thyself* pure. (1 Timothy 5:22; emphasis added)

> Pure religion and undefiled before God and the Father is this, To visit the fatherless and widows in their affliction, and to *keep himself* unspotted from the world. (James 1:27; emphasis added)

> Little children, *keep yourselves* from idols. (1 John 5:21; emphasis added)

> *Keep yourselves* in the love of God, looking for the mercy of our Lord Jesus Christ unto eternal life. (Jude 21; emphasis added)

Each of the verses above has the word "keep" in it as a reminder that God has the keeping power to cleanse us and make us pure and unspotted with a heart devoted Him. No, we won't be perfect, but we will have a heart devoted to the Lord if we really want that.

Guarding Our Hearts From Becoming Hard

I, therefore, choose to live in expectation and hope that God can do a great work in our lives even if the world is falling apart. While there is only so much each of us can do, it is important to remember that God looks at the "heart":

> Every way of a man is right in his own eyes: but the LORD pondereth the hearts. (Proverbs 21:2)

> I the LORD search the heart, I try the reins, even to give every man according to his ways, and according to the fruit of his doings. (Jeremiah 17:10)

Even if we find ourselves in situations where there is nothing we *can* do, we can always keep our hearts devoted to God—to have a heart after God's own heart as the Bible describes of the Psalmist, David (Acts 13:22).

Sometimes, when we check our hearts, we may find something there that is not fully pleasing to the Lord. Perhaps

> **Even if we find ourselves in a situation where there is nothing we can do, we can always keep our hearts devoted to God.**

we may have a very busy schedule, but then we take a moment in our day to stop and reflect on what's happening in our heart. Jesus was grieved at the hardness of heart He witnessed in His day. For example, in Mark 3, Jesus entered a synagogue on the Sabbath where there was a man with a "withered hand." The Pharisees watched for an opportunity to accuse Jesus, and He knew the condition of their hearts:

> And [Jesus] saith unto them, Is it lawful to do good on the sabbath days, or to do evil? to save life, or to kill? . . . [And He] looked round about on them with anger, being grieved for the hardness of their hearts. (Mark 3:4-5)

Actually, Jesus had much to say about the condition of our hearts. The heart is basically the wellspring of our deep-seated emotions, convictions, and beliefs that incite us into action. We see this happening (again in Mark 3) where we read of the reaction of the Pharisees after Jesus healed the man:

> And the Pharisees went forth, and straightway took counsel with the Herodians against him, how they might destroy him. (Mark 3:6)

Jesus points out that our actions are a reflection of what is happening in our hearts:

> A good man out of the good treasure of the heart bringeth forth good things: and an evil man out of the evil treasure bringeth forth evil things. (Matthew 12:35)

In response to the mandate of the scribes and Pharisees to wash one's hands before eating bread, Jesus said:

> This people draweth nigh unto me with their mouth, and honoureth me with their lips; but their heart is far from me.

> . . . teaching for doctrines the commandments of men . . . Do not ye yet understand, that whatsoever entereth in at the mouth goeth into the belly, and is cast out into the draught? But those things which proceed out of the mouth come forth from the heart; and they defile the man. For out of the heart proceed evil thoughts, murders, adulteries, fornications, thefts, false witness, blasphemies: These are the things which defile a man: but to eat with unwashen hands defileth not a man. (Matthew 15:8-9, 17-20; emphasis added)

People today are being overwhelmed with a multitude of worries and cares. The remedies the world offers are oftentimes worse than the original problems themselves (as we saw with Covid). We, as Christians, are affected by these things, and it is a temptation to put our focus on the challenges and trials, while the real solution lies in allowing Jesus Christ to be the center of our lives through His Word and His Spirit.

Above all, let us remember what it means for Christ to be our foundation and the spiritual Rock from which we can drink. We need to draw our strength from Him and remember that our virtue comes from Him as well. Christ is our all in all. That is why Paul could say, "But of him are ye in Christ Jesus, who of God is made unto us wisdom, and righteousness, and sanctification, and redemption: that, according as it is written, He that glorieth, let him glory in the Lord" (1 Corinthians 1:30-31).

It takes a humble heart to recognize that all our own righteousness is as filthy rags, but He can clothe us with the "garments of salvation . . . [and] the robe of righteousness" (Isaiah 61:10).

Where Our Treasure Lies

As committed Christians, should we not want our treasures to be in Heaven and in the things of the Lord? Remember Paul's exhortation:

> If ye then be risen with Christ, seek those things which are above, where Christ sitteth on the right hand of God. (Colossians 3:1)

The following from Luke reiterates Matthew 12:35:

> A good man out of the good treasure of his heart bringeth forth that which is good; and an evil man out of the evil treasure of his heart bringeth forth that which is evil: for of the abundance of the heart his mouth speaketh. (Luke 6:45)

Jesus' use of the word "treasure" is quite informative because it adds another attribute to what and where our heart is. In another place, He said, "For where your treasure is, there will your heart be also" (Matthew 6:21).

The Greek word for heart is *kardia* meaning literally our physical heart, which is at the core or center of our bodies, but it is continually used figuratively, just as we do in English. The Hebrew word for heart also has the same literal and figurative meaning that signifies at the core of who we really are is also the place we find the things we truly treasure. As believers in Christ, we should always hope that God has a special place there—should I say has all of our heart, for when Jesus summarized the intent of the whole Law, He said:

> The first of all the commandments is, Hear, O Israel; The Lord our God is one Lord: And thou shalt love the Lord thy God *with all thy heart,* and with all thy soul, and with all thy mind, and with all thy strength: this is the first commandment. And the second is like, namely this, Thou shalt love thy neighbour as thyself. There is none other commandment greater than these. (Mark 12: 29-31; emphasis added)

Unfortunately, most of the scribes and Pharisees had lost the intent of the Law and turned it from a heart issue to a vast array of dos and don'ts.

Please keep in mind also that "keeping" or "guarding" our hearts has a lot more to do than just protecting ourselves. It really has to do with keeping our heart in the right place as we treasure the things that are truly most important. For Jesus, the most important matter on His heart was the salvation of souls, and for that, He, who was a sinless unblemished Lamb, gave the ultimate sacrifice—His own life.

> The fence of neutrality is being shaken where we are now often forced to take a stand.

Now as we witness an unprecedented number of challenges throughout today's society, our whole world has become a testing ground for where people will place their hearts; will it be for the things of God or for vain or wicked purposes? The fence of neutrality is being shaken where we are now often forced to take a stand. Along with these challenges, we have witnessed the forces of good and evil, accompanied with truth and falsehood, pulling at our heartstrings, so to speak, and bringing confusion to our minds.

And now, in the present moment, as I write this chapter, we face one of the biggest challenges of all because it is something very dear to God's own heart—and that is Israel. God chose Israel from all the nations of the world to be His special possession. In an interview pertaining to the Hamas massacre in Israel on October 7, 2023, an Israeli man spoke to a pastor of his deeply felt appreciation for Christians who have not been bought out by the lies and false media concerning the Jews.[1] But he added a strong word of caution in saying that, even the devotion of Christians who stand behind Israel will be severely tested. After the attack on Israel, it didn't take too long before mainstream media began blocking and ignoring accurate information in favor of lies; and pro-Palestinian, pro-Hamas protests began erupting around the world denouncing Israel's existence as a nation and her right to defend herself against terrorist attacks. Even many claiming to be in the Christian camp began denouncing Israel. And so, the testing of our hearts begins again, but this time concerning the apple of God's eye.

> For the LORD's portion is his people; Jacob is the lot of his inheritance. He found him in a desert land, and in the waste howling wilderness; he led him about, he instructed him, he kept him as the apple of his eye. (Deuteronomy 32:9-10)

In these times of testing and challenge, let us guard our hearts with all diligence, knowing that as we keep our eyes on Him and our hope in Him, He will be our strength:

> Be of good courage, and he shall strengthen your heart, all ye that hope in the LORD. (Psalm 31:24)

Epilogue

Psalm 23—
The Faithfulness of God

> The Lord is my shepherd; I shall not want.

When David penned the words to Psalm 23, he attested in unquestioning words to the faithfulness of God. Verse 1 is one of the boldest statements found in Scripture because it testifies to the faithfulness of God from a man who had a unique relationship with the Lord. Here was a man after God's own heart, a man who grew to believe that God is always faithful no matter what our position in life may be. God is glorious, and never can too much be said to the glory and majesty of God. Or as Jeremiah so aptly put it, "This I recall to my mind, therefore have I hope. It is of the LORD's mercies that we are not consumed, because his compassions fail not. They are new every morning: great is thy faithfulness" (Lamentations 3:21-23). God's mercies are enduring.

So let us listen as David takes up his melodic harp. In verse 1, with song unwavering, David proclaims his trust and enduring assurance to the faithfulness of God. David had been a meek shepherd who watched his flocks day after day, caring for them. He knew that God is a shepherd too, looking after His own. What a wonderful God we have. And just as he cared for all of the needs of his flock, David looked to his Lord to be the provider for all of his needs. Verse 1, "The LORD is my shepherd; I shall not want," is a summation statement of all that follows in this psalm; yet this verse comes at the beginning rather than the end because each succeeding verse carries with it his resolute declaration to the faithfulness of God as the loving Shepherd who attends to all of the needs of His flock throughout our entire lifespan. Psalm 23 takes us through the sojourn the shepherd takes with his sheep to the mountain pastures and then back home again. I hope to describe the tone and testament to God's character presented in this psalm.

> He maketh me to lie down in green pastures: he leadeth me beside the still waters.

Verse 2 then carries the message of God's faithfulness found in verse 1 and renders it like the softer chords of a melody, alluding to the quiet love of the shepherd as he leads his sheep to green pastures bathed in the beauty of gently warming sunlight and soft breezes like a hand brushing over the tops of these slender grasses. To such a place, the shepherd brings his sheep to lay down if but for a little while to be renewed in the quiet confidence that gives strength—not so much in the physical event itself as in knowing and believing that the shepherd is there to sustain them. The shepherd then bids his sheep to come to the still waters; but more so than a bidding, he literally leads them to the still waters, which remind me so much of the living water Jesus offered to the woman He met at the well. The Word of God is life giving, like water to one who thirsts, in that it brings us to Jesus who is in the truest sense that living water springing up to eternal life. Notice again it says that the shepherd "leads." The great wonder of the Christian faith is that it brings us to the Shepherd of our souls whose purpose is to guide us every step along our life-long journey. There can be no greater and truer comfort than knowing that Jesus is there guiding us. This quiet confidence is available to all who would be so bold as to yield their lives to Jesus by faith—trusting not in their ability to follow Him but in His ability to lead us. As the Scriptures say both implicitly and literally throughout the Bible, "the just shall live by faith" (Romans 1:17), so too it is by faith that the Lord leads us. This is one of the great proclamations of this psalm—the Lord leads me; and He does so as we put our confidence in Him (not in ourselves) to do so.

> **He restoreth my soul: he leadeth me in the paths of righteousness for his name's sake.**

Like the strummings of a melodic harp, we can hear the chords of restoration. Yes, there is nothing like spending the day under the watchful eye of the Shepherd of our souls. When we come to Him, He renews us and strengthens us. Nothing can really be compared to the work of regeneration God performs in us when we come to Jesus the first time; we are truly born from above at that time. Yet, Jesus then abides in us to continually renew and strengthen us. If you are a Christian who is feeling weary from the testings and trials of life, be assured that Jesus is knocking at your heart's door to speak words of hope and comfort. Our journey may be difficult at times, but Jesus is there to renew us and bid us to go on. And on we go, from the pasture lands that feed us and the waters that restore our thirsty souls, on we go up into the hills. As Christians, no matter what station of life we are in, God has a call on each of our lives, and simply put, that call is to follow

Him. And it is on the paths of righteousness that He leads us. Too often, we as Christians would want to get what we can out of life. There is the temptation to be selfish and self-centered. But God leads us on the paths of righteousness for His name's sake. Our very lives should be a testament to the goodness and faithfulness of God. Today, there is much sin within God's own flock. Let us remember that even though we are justified by the shed blood of Jesus alone, by faith alone, the fruit of our salvation should reflect the nature of God in our own character. That is why Paul said that the sins of immorality and ungodliness should not be named among us (Ephesians 5:3). As believers, we are being refined and renewed by the Holy Spirit who changes us continually "from glory to glory" (2 Corinthians 3:18).

> Yea, though I walk through the valley of the shadow of death, I will fear no evil: for thou art with me; thy rod and thy staff they comfort me.

Verse 4 proclaims the secret for knowing God's peace. One of the ironies of life is that those who have known suffering are oftentimes the very ones who have found the lasting peace that can only come from Christ alone. Here the psalmist declares his abiding faith, refined by God's testings, by saying he will not fear even under the shadow of death. David's melodic harp continues on, and though the word "death" would ordinarily strike fear in the heart, somehow the music continues with beautiful chords beckoning our hearts to be still and witness the beauty of the Lord in the more trying moments of life. Up through the shadowy crags, the shepherd leads his sheep where predators often hide awaiting the moment when they can spring upon their victims. Yet, we learn here the secret of perfect peace in knowing that

Psalm 23—The Faithfulness of God

though danger may be near, and only God knows the outcome, we have hope and assurance that God is with us. The sheep know no fear when they know the shepherd is near; their hope and trust is that explicit. Is there any reason why we should not trust our Lord that fully? And, if there is a reason, what would that reason be?

His rod and staff, which are symbols of both his authority and ownership of the sheep, are also weapons of warfare, and hence bring a deep sense of comfort especially in this place of danger. Isn't it true that God, who is mighty to correct and reprove His children, can by that same attribute bring comfort and peace as we know that no real harm can ever come to God's people who put their trust in Him? Remember Jesus said: "Be not afraid of them that kill the body, and after that have no more that they can do. But I will forewarn you whom ye shall fear: Fear him, which after he hath killed hath power to cast into hell; yea, I say unto you, Fear him" (Luke 12:4-5). Unfortunately, the fear of the Lord is being robbed from our present generation of young people. "New" spirituality leaders have converged on them like wolves in sheep's clothing encouraging them to break away from the moral restraints presented in Scripture as well as from teachings on salvation that show how we are justified by faith through the sacrificial death of Jesus on the Cross. The negative result from all of this is that our young people are being scattered from the watchful care of the *true* Shepherd only to have false teachers spring on them with all of their mortally toxic teachings.

I am so grateful that David, who was a good shepherd to his flock, became a shepherd to his people and pointed the way for us to see the true Shepherd of our souls. And here, there is great comfort in knowing God as He really is and trusting Him fully.

> Thou preparest a table before me in the presence of mine enemies: thou anointest my head with oil; my cup runneth over.

The melodic music continues from the harp, not halting or wavering from its beautiful tones, as the psalm continues in its stirring message. The shepherd has now brought his sheep up through the cliffs and crags of the mountainside to a "table" where the sheep can stop again and feed on the gentle grasses. Though the enemy yet lurks on the fringes of this plateau, the shepherd's watchful eye keeps them safe. They proceed to graze again while the shepherd tends to the sheep individually, bearing his horn filled with healing oil. What a blessing it is to know the care of the shepherd, anointing his sheep with healing oil. I also appreciate the fact that, while the last verse speaks of "the shadow of death," this one speaks of renewal. We all face the prospect of something negative happening to us or to those we care for, whether it be death itself or some kind of loss that makes our hopes and dreams seem unreachable and brings them to a grinding halt. But this verse demonstrates that we can go through the valley and come out on the other side. The strings of the harp now plucked to their most vibrant sound speak of those moments in life where perhaps all seems lost, but then renewed hope rings out with a new beginning or a way in which to go. It is the most joyous sound that speaks of God's ability to take a difficult situation and bring light out of darkness and joy out of sorrow.

Psalm 23—The Faithfulness of God

> **Surely goodness and mercy shall follow me all the days of my life: and I will dwell in the house of the LORD for ever.**

Now we come to the sweet refrain upon the harp. We return to the familiar pastures we call home. As if boasting before all who will hear, the sheep testify to the goodness and mercy of the Lord—whose mercies are new every morning; but also in their yearly transhumance,* the sheep return to winter in their pastoral home on the valley below. If we boast, let us boast in the Lord, and this psalm is a vibrant proclamation to the faithful care of our Good Shepherd throughout the days of our lives. Surely, the joy in life is in knowing that we will dwell in the house of the Lord forever, and we can know the joy of salvation even now.

The music has now ended as the tone of the vibrating harp-strings fades away. No doubt, this was a song of rare beauty as we have as our witness words unrivaled by songwriter or poet. Yet, there is something even more precious to behold than mere words and melody in that this psalm is a testament to the relationship David had with his Lord that would be difficult for a commentator or theologian to adequately describe. And that is the matter that David was a man after God's own heart; yet in this psalm, David invites us to enter into that same relationship with our Lord; there is no formula or code here, no ten-step plan—but an abiding relationship that comes from having a heart after God.

I should note here that God uses the difficulties that come our way in life to shape our character, but most importantly, He wants us to draw close to Him. The fruit of staying near to the Shepherd, if we allow Him to do His work in us, is that we have a heart after God. This is a place of staying close to Him, of being led by God on

---

*Seasonal movement of livestock (such as sheep) between mountain and lowland pastures under the care of herders. (*Webster*)

a daily basis. Are you aware of God orchestrating your life? By faith, you can trust Him to lead you on a daily basis, for the Word of God says "the just shall live by faith" (Romans 1:17). That means we can and should be trusting Him to lead us by the power of the Holy Spirit on a daily basis. It is a journey on the paths of righteousness, past the meadows and quiet streams of renewal through reading His Word, up through the valleys of difficulties, to the table of restoration for summer feeding, then back to winter pastures in the valley below. God should be involved in the details of our lives throughout the year. For the Christian, there is no vacation from God, but at the same time, there is no better, no safer place, than to be near to God. Do you have a thirst for God? Seek after Him, with the Bible daily in your hands, and ask the Lord to lead you. The Holy Spirit is given to believers to be our Shepherd and guide through life with all its dangers and challenges. And as we come to trust Him more and more, drawing near to Him with every challenge we face, we will find that we too have a heart after God like David did.

Endnotes

Chapter 3: Sound the Trumpet in the Midst of Apostasy
1. For a history of Lighthouse Trails, read our article "The Story Behind Lighthouse Trails" online at http://www.lighthousetrailsresearch.com/blog/?p=15423 or order it in the booklet format.
2. See *A Time of Departing* for more information on Alice Bailey's "revitalization" of the churches.
3. *Beware the Bridgers* is available for free in CD through Lighthouse Trails.
4. The two men discussed in this section are Todd Friel and John MacArthur's Executive Director Phil Johnson speaking at the 2011 Psalm 119 Conference in Keller, TX (you can watch this segment of the conference where "discernment divas" are talked about at: https://web.archive.org/web/20111026163305/http://teampyro.blogspot.com/2011/10/first-blast-of-trumpet-against.html).
5. Though Deborah Dombrowski's name was not mentioned, it was inferred by saying Lighthouse Trails Publishing as at the time, she was the only woman writer for Lighthouse Trails.

Chapter 4: The P.E.A.C.E. of Man versus the Peace of God
1. Alice Bailey, *Problems of Humanity* (New York, NY: Lucis Publishing, 1993), p. 152.
2. Alice Bailey, *The Externalization of the Hierarchy* (New York, NY: Lucis Publishing, 1976), p. 510.
3. See Roger Oakland's report, *A Christian Perspective on Environmentalism* and Tony Pearce's report, *Global Warming or Cooling or an End-Time Sign?* Both on the Lighthouse Trails Research site.
4. At the Pew Forum in 2005, Rick Warren said: "You know, 500 years ago, the first Reformation with Luther and then Calvin, was about beliefs. I think a new reformation is going to be about behavior.

The first Reformation was about creeds [doctrine]; I think this one will be about deeds. I think the first one was about what the church believes; I think this one will be about what the church does. The first Reformation actually split Christianity into dozens and then hundreds of different segments. I think this one is actually going to bring them together." (Pew Research Center, May 23, 2005, https://www.pewresearch.org/religion/2005/05/23/myths-of-the-modern-megachurch/)

Chapter 5: Signs & Wonders
1. Roger Oakland, *The Good Shepherd Calls* (Roseburg, OR: Lighthouse Trails Publishing, 2017), p. 97.

Chapter 6: Drugs, Meditation, & "A Fully Developed Spirituality"
1. Nanci Des Gerlaise addresses this issue of cultures in *Muddy Waters* and also in her booklet *Can Cultures Be Redeemed?* Both available through Lighthouse Trails and on Amazon.

2.. Roger Oakland, *Faith Undone* (Roseburg, OR: Lighthouse Trails Publishing, 2007), p. 98.

3. Ibid., p. 99; citing Richard Foster, *Prayer: Finding the Heart's True Home* (San Francisco, CA: Harper, 1992, First Edition), p. 157.

4. Napolean A. Chagnon, *Yanomamo: The Fierce People* (New York, NY: Holt, Reinhart and Winston, 3rd edition), pp.112-113.

5. A statement by Matthew Fox who was quoting Thomas Merton from a statement Merton told him in 1967 (http://web.archive.org/web/20060425035122/nineoclockservice.tripod.com/mattiefx.htm).

6. Read Warren Smith's book *False Christ Coming: Does Anybody Care?* or his online article at https://www.lighthousetrailsresearch.com/blog/?p=15611) discussing the "Selection Process."

7. Neale Donald Walsch, *The New Revelations: A Conversation with God* (New York, NY: Atria Books, 2002), p. 157.

8. Richard Kirby, *The Mission of Mysticism* (London, UK: SPCK, 1979), p. 7. as cited in *A Time of Departing*, 2nd ed., p. 32.

9. David Steindl-Rast, "Recollection of Thomas Merton's Last Days in the West" (*Monastic Studies,* 7:10, 1969).

10. Alice Bailey, *Problems of Humanity* (New York, NY: Lucis Publishing, 1993), p. 152.

11. Ray Yungen, *A Time of Departing* (Roseburg, OR: Lighthouse Trails Publishing, 2nd edition, 2006), p. 124.

12. Yungen states: "The term 'vibrationally sympathetic' here means those who suspend thought through word repetition or breath focus—inward mental silence. That is what attracts them. That is their opening. That is why New Ager Tilden Edwards called this the 'bridge to far Eastern spirituality,' and this is what is being injected into the evangelical church!" (*A Time of Departing,* 2nd ed., p. 88). According to quantum spirituality, desirable changes can occur when a sufficient number of people are meditating, thereby achieving "critical mass." Those who refuse to meditate will be seen as impeding this progress by not being "vibrationally sympathetic."

Chapter 7: Calvinism, Catholicism, or Blessed Assurance

1. *My Journey Out of Catholicism* is David's testimonial booklet. You may read it online at https://www.lighthousetrailsresearch.com/blog/?p=10964.

2. Bernard Cottret, *Calvin: A Biography* (Grand Rapids, MI: Eerdmans Pub. Company, English translation, 2000). See also Bob Kirkland, *Calvinism: None Dare Call It Heresy* (Roseburg, OR: Lighthouse Trails Publishing, 2018).

3. Harry Ironside, *Should Christians Expose Error?* (https://www.lighthousetrailsresearch.com/blog/?p=18549).

4. Read Mike Oppenheimer's booklet, *Understanding Paul's Appeal at Mars Hill* (https://www.lighthousetrailsresearch.com/blog/?p=13357).

5. Norman F. Douty, *The Death of Christ* (Irving, TX: Williams & Watrous Pub. Co., Revised and Enlarged Edition, 1978), p. 176, citing John Calvin from F. F. Bruce's "Answers and Questions," Question 1331, in *The Harvester* (Exeter) January 1966.

6. Ray Yungen, "The Desert Fathers—Borrowing From the East" (https://www.lighthousetrailsresearch.com/blog/?p=30353).

7. A.W. Pink, *The Sovereignty of God.* (This theme that no one can resist God's will is throughout Pink's book.)

8. R. C. Sproul, "Assurance of Salvation" (*Tabletalk,* Ligonier Ministries, Inc., 1989), p. 20; cited from Dave Hunt's book, *What*

Love is This? (Bend, OR: The Berean Call, 2013, 4th edition), from chapter 29, endnote #25.

Chapter 8: A Potter Looks at Romans 9
1. You can watch this video presentation at: https://www.youtube.com/watch?v=IBADZEz2n3g.

Chapter 9: Legalism vs. License or the Treasure of Living Water
1. To understand more about the emerging church and emergent views, read Roger Oakland's article, "How to Know When the Emerging Church Shows Signs of Emerging Into Your Church" at: https://www.lighthousetrailsresearch.com/blog/?p=11043; also in booklet format.

2. Harry Ironside, *Changed by Beholding* (Roseburg, OR: Lighthouse Trails Publishing, 2018 edition), pp. 14-16. You can read more by Harry Ironside by visiting www.harryironside.com.

Chapter 10: Hard Lessons in Discernment
1. "So You Still Think *The Chosen* Is an Accurate Reflection of the "Authentic" Jesus Christ? Really?" (https://www.lighthousetrailsresearch.com/blog/?p=35080).

2. "A Critique of *The Chosen* Season 1 & 2" (https://www.youtube.com/watch?v=xTh3glbl8s4).

3. Dallas Jenkins often says that the fictionalized stories he's created are "plausible." According to *Webster's Dictionary*, the word plausible means "superficially fair, reasonable, or valuable but often specious (i.e., having a "false look of truth or genuineness" and "having deceptive attraction or allure").

4. "Video Critique: *The Chosen*—Calling John the Baptist "Creepy John" and Jesus and John the Baptist Arguing About Herod" (https://www.lighthousetrailsresearch.com/blog/?p=34616).

5. "A Candid Conversation with Dallas Jenkins, Director of *The Chosen*" (Melissa Dougherty, 4/27/21, https://www.youtube.com/watch?v=__-Yyq1FPQI), mm: 67:45-67:55.

6. Ibid., mm: 25:11.

7. "Interview with a Mormon and an Evangelical!" (https://www.youtube.com/watch?v=SXIiv3NhIhc&t=796s), mm: 9:37-10:55.

Chapter 14: Neglecting to Test the Spirits
1. Brennan Manning, *Above All* (Brentwood, TN: Integrity Publishers, 2003), pp. 58-59, as quoted from Roger Oakland in *Faith Undone*, p. 195.
2. Ray Yungen, *A Time of Departing*, op. cit., p. 94.
3. William Shannon, *Silence on Fire* (New York, NY: The Crossroad Publishing Company, 1995 edition), pp. 109-110.
4. Henri Nouwen, *Sabbatical Journey* (New York, NY: The Crossroad Publishing Company, 1998 Hardcover edition), p. 51.
5. Basil Pennington, *Centering Prayer* (Garden City, NY: Image Book edition, 1982) pp. 220-221.
6. Thomas Keating, *Intimacy with God* (New York, NY: Crossroad, 1994), p. 153.
7. Brennan Manning, *The Signature of Jesus* (Sisters, OR: Multnomah, 1996, Revised Edition), p. 215.
8. Sometime in late 2018 or early 2019, the endorsement page on the Jesus Calling website was removed. Lighthouse Trails editors e-mailed HarperCollins and asked what happened to the endorsement page. We were told it was down temporarily for re-designing but would be put back up. To date, that page is still missing, but we have heard of no Christian leader from the endorsement page who has spoken up warning about *Jesus Calling* or retracting his or her endorsement. You can find an archived link of this page here: https://web.archive.org/web/20181205214012/https://www.jesuscalling.com/media/endorsements.
9. Sarah Young, *Jesus Calling: Enjoying Peace in His Presence,* 10th Anniversary Edition (Nashville, TN; Thomas Nelson Inc, 2004, 2011, 2014), p. 66.
10. Ibid.
11. Warren B. Smith, *"Another Jesus" Calling,* 2nd ed. (Mountain Stream Press, 2016), pp. 53-54.
12. Richard Foster, *Prayer: Finding the Heart's True Home* (San Francisco, CA: Harper,1992, First Edition), p. 157.

13. Ibid.
14. Ibid.
15. Ibid., p. 156.
16. Ibid.
17. Richard Foster, *Celebration of Discipline* (San Francisco, CA: Harper & Row, 1978 edition), p. 13.
18. Roger Oakland, "Richard Foster's Contemplative Prayer or Contemplative Terror?" (https://www.lighthousetrailsresearch.com/blog/richard-fosters-contemplative-prayer-or-contemplative-terror/); also an extract from Oakland's book *Faith Undone,* pp. 99-101.
19. Mike Oppenheimer, "Understanding the Premise of Contemplative" (http://www.letusreason.org/Popteach80.htm).

Chapter 15: Guard Your Heart With All Diligence

1. "War in Israel" (October 2023, https://www.youtube.com/watch?v=J79vX-D-tjs&t=1030s).

INDEX

A

abiding faith 200
abortion 38
Abraham 16, 114, 119, 120, 122
absolution 15
age of Aquarius 78, 82
   enlightenment 80
   peace 78, 80
   peace and oneness 78
all embracing silence 181
altar call 13, 96, 112
altered state of consciousness 73, 77, 181
America 4, 49, 52, 70, 155-156
Anabaptists 14, 89
angels of light 77, 80
animal-like behaviors 61
another gospel 19, 20, 112, 158
anthropology 70, 75, 80
antichrist / Antichrist 38-39, 47, 61-62, 66, 81, 99-100, 134, 172
antisemitism 38, 47, 62
apostasy 35-37, 48, 51-52, 62-63, 101, 133, 149-150, 171, 173-174, 183-184

apparitions of Mary 60
Ark of the Covenant 186
assurance of salvation 87, 97-98 106, 112
A Time of Departing 35, 76
atonement 81, 118, 156, 172-173
atoning, redemptive work of Christ on the Cross 179
Augustine 89, 91

B

Babylon 78, 80, 82
Bailey, Alice 37, 47, 80-82
Baltimore Catechism 15
baptism 176
also see infant baptism
Bethlehem 142
Bible colleges and seminaries *see* Christian colleges
Bible prophecy 27, 39, 47, 172
Book of Mormon 137-138
breath prayers 162, 176
bridgers 39, 40
Buddhism 22, 81
Bunyan, John 126

Editor's Note: Certain words, such as Gospel, salvation, and discernment, that are used extensively throughout the book are not in this index.

C

Calvary 93, 96, 100, 106, 121
Calvin, John 87-89, 91-93, 95, 97-98, 106-107, 110-113
Calvinism 41, 85, 87-89, 91, 93 94-95, 97-98, 103, 106-107, 111-113, 115
Canada 49
Canadian Native peoples 69
Catholic charismatic movement 20, 132
Catholicism / Catholic Church 13-14, 18-22, 46-47, 60, 85, 89, 92, 96, 101, 105, 113, 132, 148
   confessing sins to a priest 15
   Mass 18-19, 20-21, 85, 96
   monks 73
   "Mother Church" 39
   sacrament of the Eucharist 15, 20, 85, 93, 96-97, 106
   the sacraments 15, 96
   theologians 144
   transubstantiation 149
centering prayer 175-176
   see also contemplative spirituality
chanting 74, 77
Chief Shoefoot 70, 72-74, 78-79
   see also shamanism
"Christ" consciousness 148
Christian colleges and seminaries 36, 62, 87, 89, 117, 173
Christian leaders 37, 40, 49, 51, 58, 134, 149, 159, 162, 173, 175, 177, 183, 186
Christian publishers 36, 173

church fathers 92
climate change 48, 172
Cloud, Henry 177
communion wafers 60
Communist party 28-29
contemplative spirituality 24, 29, 35, 37-39, 72-74, 76-81, 117, 132, 158, 162, 174-176, 180-182
contemplative terror 181
convulsions 61
Covid 150-151, 153, 187-188, 191
creation 48, 111, 138, 169
Creator 50, 53, 67, 109, 169
Cree and Saulteaux tribes 69
"creeping" effect 173
critical mass 82
Cross, the 13-16, 25-26, 28, 33-34, 65, 71, 81-82, 85, 92, 112-113, 126, 148-149, 162, 167, 170
cult 23
curse of the Law 121-122

D

day of Pentecost 64
deliverance rituals 132
Des Gerlaise, Nanci 69
Desert Fathers 29, 73
devotion to Mary 46
dismantling of the Gospel 134
Dittman, Anita 157
   see also Holocaust
"divine center" 29, 39
doctrines of devils 57
dominionism 46-47, 51, 53
drugs 18, 21, 27, 69, 74, 77, 79-80

Index

E

earthquakes 39, 48, 151
eastern gurus 61
eastern meditative practices 29, 38, 76
eastern religions 27
economic collapse 155
economic forces 38
ecumenism 22, 149, 151, 171
emergent / emerging church 24, 29, 36, 47, 117, 124, 148, 181
emerging progressive leaders 47, 168
end times 48-49, 78, 79
energy healing practices 38
enlightened consciousness 76
esoteric experiences 117, 149
eternal life 19, 102, 106, 145-146, 199
eternal security 94, 98
  see also assurance of salvation
Eucharist 15, 18, 20, 46, 85, 93, 96-97, 103, 106
  see also Catholicism
Eves, Derral 135
  see also The Chosen
evil spirits 74
experience-driven Christianity 172
experiential "gospel" 53
extremes 118, 150
extreme weather conditions 172

F

faithfulness of God 197-198, 200
Faith Undone 74, 180
false christs 39, 57, 134, 158
false leaders and prophets 59
false prophets 57, 175, 178, 187

fasting 74
fatalism 94, 103
fatalistic viewpoint 107
father of lies 58
first pope 92
floods 48, 146-147
foreknowledge 114
Foster, Richard 74, 180-182
free will 94-95, 106, 109-111, 113-114
fruit of the Spirit 32
fundamentals of the Christian faith 168

G

Gentiles 114, 121, 162
Germany 17, 47, 62, 86, 132, 157
global
  currency 38
  leaders 47
  peace 47, 50
  thinkers 151
  unity 151
  warming 48
gossip 131
grace 15-16, 18-19, 59-60, 71, 99, 101, 103, 113, 117, 127, 163-164
Graham, Jack 177
grand delusion 39
Groeschel, Craig 177

H

Hamas 193-194
  see also antisemitism
hatred toward Bible-believing born-again believers 38

heart of man 16, 114
Heaven 16, 51, 58-59, 65, 88, 92, 94, 97, 135, 148
Hegelian Formula 88
Hell 14-15, 58, 88, 94, 97-98, 100, 106, 112, 149, 168
highly evolved society 37
Hinduism 22
Hippie movement 27, 79
Hitler, Adolph 42, 47, 62, 86, 95
holiness 126-127, 146
Holocaust, the 157
Holy Communion 113
   see also Catholicism
holy laughter 61
Hunt, Dave 115
hypnotic state 79

Jewish history 86
Jewish people 145-146
Jews, the 50, 90, 121
John the Baptist 47, 63, 135-137
Jones, Alan 29
judgment 17, 48-49, 65, 82, 110, 155-157
justified by faith 18-19, 26, 111, 120, 162, 164, 179, 201

K
Keating, Thomas 175-176
kingdom-now
   see dominionism
Kirkland, Bob 115
Kundalini energy 61

I
indigenous peoples of the world 71
infant baptism 14, 89, 96
inner healing 132
inquisition in Geneva 89
interfaith ecumenism 149
Ironside, Harry 88-89, 125
Israel 30, 59, 64, 108, 110, 142, 149, 166, 192-194

L
lectio divina 162
legalism 117, 124, 127
livestock 203
LSD 79
   see also drugs
Lucado, Max 177
lying wonders 62

J
Japan earthquake, tsunami 48,
Jenkins, Dallas 131, 135, 137-139
   see also The Chosen
Jeremiah, David 177
jerkings 61
Jesus Calling 138, 176-177
Jesus Movement 27

M
Machiavelli 188
manifestations 60-62, 65-66
man-made disasters 39
Manning, Brennan 172, 174, 176
mantra 74, 77, 79
marijuana 18, 79
   see also drugs
Mars Hill 90
martyrdom 49

Index

Marx Hubbard, Barbara 80
Mask-e-pe-toon 70
Mass
  see Catholicism
McLaren, Brian 29
media, mainstream 48, 193-194
Medieval thought 89
meditation 29, 69, 73, 76, 80-82
mercy 67, 69, 77, 113, 115, 127, 203
Merton, Thomas 21, 73, 79, 81, 174-175, 182
metamodern 172, 185
Middle Ages 73
Millard, Bart 177
mind-altering drugs 79
meditation 158
  techniques 92
missionary efforts 70
mission organizations 71
Mormonism 135, 137-138
Mosaic Law 145
Mother Teresa 17
mystical paradigm shift 57
mystical practices 35, 39, 73, 77, 79, 156, 162
mysticism 24, 29, 33, 37, 73, 76-81, 96, 171, 174, 179, 182

N

Nathan, Richard and Linda 79
national "repentance" 156
Native Spirituality 76-77
natural disasters 39, 48, 155
Nazi Germany 157
New Age 29, 33, 37, 40, 45, 47, 57, 72-73, 76, 78, 80-82, 96, 148-149, 151, 171, 174
New Age P.E.A.C.E. plan 45
New Missiology 71
"new" quantum science 168
new spirituality 173-174
"New" spirituality leaders 201
new world/new reformation 80
new-world order 151
Nicodemus 19
Nouwen, Henri 21, 174-175, 182
nuclear attack 155
nuclear holocaust 48
nuclear threat 172

O

Oakland, Roger 66, 71, 74, 180
occult 37, 73, 76-77, 81, 112
occultic 40, 57, 74, 77, 79, 81, 158
occultic practices 37, 57, 76
occultic prayer 81
occultic realm 77, 79
occultism 80
oneness 78, 80
one-world
  global order 37
  government 172
  order 38
  thinkers 151

P

pandemic 38, 150, 153
panentheistic 73, 96, 169
pantheistic 73, 96
parables 19, 51, 104-105, 107
paradigm shift 57, 173
paranormal manifestation 61

participation in Holy
    Communion 113
    see also Catholicism
pastors 22, 25, 28-29, 40, 54,
    117, 171, 173-175, 177,
    183, 186
P.E.A.C.E. of Man 45
peace on Earth 46
P.E.A.C.E. plan 38, 45
peace plans 54
peace, purpose, and prosperity 49
peace with God 59, 162, 164
Pearce, Tony 205
pedophilia 38
penal substitutionary atonement 172
Pennington, Basil 73, 175-177, 180
perfecting of the saints 170
persecution 46, 49, 53, 82, 90, 105, 157
"perseverance of the saints" 113
    see also Calvinism
Pink, A.W. 95
    see also Calvinism
Poland 13, 85-86, 101
politically correct 71
pornography 28-29
postmodernism 49, 168, 172-173, 185
potter's field 166
power of God 25, 30, 34, 66, 72, 90-91, 162
power of the Law 120-121
predestination 87, 97, 107
preparedness 159, 160, 164
preterism 47

priesthood of all believers 149
progressivism 47, 71, 124, 127, 168, 171-173, 185
prophecy 27, 39, 47, 152, 172
prosperity prophets 157
prostitution 18
Protestant leaders 24
Purpose Driven 24, 26, 38, 45, 53, 155
    see also Warren, Rick

Q

quantum leap 173-174
quantum spirituality 81

R

Reformation, the 89
Reformed church 112
    see also Calvinism
regeneration 199
"regeneration of the churches" 80
    see also Bailey, Alice
Reiki 38, 76
relaxation exercises 162
religious forces 38
repentance 26, 42, 47-48, 51-54, 71, 110-111, 151, 156
resurrection 59, 71
revival 51, 92, 149, 156
road to Damascus 168
Rogers, Adrian 115
Roman Catholic
    see Catholicism
Roman occupation 145

S

"sacred space" 176

Index

Saddleback Church 26
   see also Warren, Rick
Samaritan woman at the well 92, 123
sanctification 91, 139-140, 191
Saulteaux tribes 69
saving grace 101, 171
Schlueter, Ingrid 40-41
"science falsely so called" 167-169
seducing spirits 57, 177
seeker-friendly 25-27
Selection Process 80
   see also Marx Hubbard, Barbara
Sermon on the Mount 137
servant leader 173
Seventh Day Adventists 144
shamanism 73, 81
Shannon, William 174
   see also Merton, Thomas
signs and wonders 39, 57-59, 60-66
silence, the 73, 77, 175, 182
simplicity of the Gospel 36, 90, 93, 102, 162
slaying in the Spirit 61, 132
Smith, Warren B. 177
social gospel 26-27, 171
social justice 149
sorceries 79
spirit guides 76, 80
spirit of antichrist 99-100, 134, 178
spiritual disciplines 24, 29, 35, 72-74, 77, 179
   see also contemplative spirituality
Spiritual Formation 35, 158, 180

spiritual preparedness 164
spiritual warfare 36
state of "silence" 175
Sproul, R.C. 97-98
St. John of the Cross 175
Stories From Indian Wigwams and Northern Campfires 69
Strobel, Lee 177
sub-atomic level 169
substitutionary death on the Cross 173
   see also Cross, the
suffering 46, 118, 200
supernatural forces 61

T

Terkeurst, Lysa 177
terrorism 172
testings and trials 199
testing (trying) the spirits 171, 175, 177-178, 180, 183, 186
test of 1 John 4:1-3 63
The Chosen series 131, 134-139
the Law 111, 114, 120-124, 145
the "mark" 38
The Purpose Driven Life 53
   see also Warren, Rick
The Shack 53
three-legged stool 45
   see also Warren, Rick
total depravity 111
   see also Calvinism
tradition of men 167
T.U.L.I.P. 111, 113, 115
   see also Calvinism

U

unified religion 172
United Nations 38
unity 38, 49, 130, 131, 151
   see also ecumenism
unpreparedness 159

V

vain
   philosophies 169
   repetitions 77
   teachings 167
vibrationally sympathetic 82
Vietnam War 17, 27, 132
violence 21, 38, 45, 47, 75, 78, 172
virgin birth 144
volcanic activity 39

W

Warren, Kay 177
Warren, Rick 38, 45, 52
"new reformation 52
wars 39, 150, 172
watchmen 43, 171, 183-184

weather phenomena 39, 48
   see also climate change
White, Ellen G. 144
wokeism 71, 171
wolves 184
wolves in sheep's clothing 61, 103, 201
world peace 45
world's belief systems 179-180
world-wide delusion 48-49, 98
   peace plan 62
   reformation 51

Y

Y2K 159
Yungen, Ray 35, 76, 81, 173
Yanomamo people 70, 73-78
   see also shamanism
Yoga 38, 76, 158, 162
youth 18, 60, 172

TOPICAL BOOKLETS FROM LIGHTHOUSE TRAILS
—OVER 150 TO CHOOSE FROM—

The Lighthouse Trails topical Booklets are designed to share with others important truths from a biblical perspective.

What is so wonderful about these Booklets is two-fold: one, they are sold at very low prices so just about anyone can afford to buy them (with quantity orders of 6 or more of the same title, the discount is as much as 45% off retail); and two, we are told when they are being handed out, people are reading them.

Each Booklet is between 10-18 pages and is written by one of the 35 Lighthouse Trails authors. Visit www.lighthousetrails.com or request a free catalog to see a complete list of the Lighthouse Trails topical booklets.

Each Booklet is $1.95 retail with the following discounts:
6-25: $1.66; 26-50: $1.46;
51-100: $1.27; 101+: $1.07 each.
These discounts apply for quantities *of the same title*.

FULL COLOR GLOSS COVERS
5 1/2" X 8 1/2" | 10-18 PAGES
HIGH QUALITY WHITE HEAVY GLOSS PAPER

LIGHTHOUSE TRAILS PRESENTS

A "New" Narrative for a "New" World is a compilation of eight glossaries from seven different Lighthouse Trails authors. Each chapter presents terms and definitions from a specific ideology. This book has a two-fold purpose:

First, each author's included commentary draws the various chapters together and paints an overall picture—a story, if you will, of what is taking place today in the church and in the world in the spiritual landscape.

And second, the book defines and explains provocative language and terms that have deceived many. It will provide a vital resource to be used for years to come (should the Lord tarry).

Authors: Chris Lawson, Kevin Reeves, Warren B. Smith, Mary Danielsen, Carl Teichrib, Richard and Linda Nathan

256 Pages | Retail: $14.95 (quantity discounts)
ISBN: 978-1-942423-71-3 | Available through Lighthouse Trails and **most major online book outlets.**

To order additional copies of:
A Faith Worth Believing in the Last Days
Send $13.95 plus shipping to:

Lighthouse Trails Publishing
P.O. Box 307
Roseburg, Oregon 97470

For shipping costs, go to
www.lighthousetrails.com/shippingcosts.htm or:
($3.95/1 book; $6.00/2 or more books)
You may also purchase Lighthouse Trails books from
www.lighthousetrails.com.

The bulk (wholesale) rates for 10 or more copies is 40% off the retail price. For U.S. & Canada orders, call our toll-free number: 866-876-3910.
For international and all other calls: 541-391-7699

A Faith Worth Believing in the Last Days as well as other books by Lighthouse Trails Publishing, can be ordered directly through Lighthouse Trails.

For more information on the topic of this book:
Lighthouse Trails Research Project
www.lighthousetrailsresearch.com

Lighthouse Trails has a free bi-weekly/monthly e-newsletter and a quarterly subscription-based 40-page print journal. Visit www.lighthousetrailsresearch.com, or call one of the numbers above to sign up for the free e-newsletter or to subscribe to the print journal ($14/year for U.S. | $22/year for CA | $38/year for international).

www.ingramcontent.com/pod-product-compliance
Lightning Source LLC
LaVergne TN
LVHW051829080426
835512LV00018B/2784